My Lips Play Flute for the Highest

My Lips Play Flute for the Highest

Jewish Hymns and Prayers before Jesus

Torleif Elgvin

CASCADE *Books* • Eugene, Oregon

MY LIPS PLAY FLUTE FOR THE HIGHEST
Jewish Hymns and Prayers before Jesus

Cascade Books
An Imprint of Wipf and Stock Publishers
199 W. 8th Ave., Suite 3
Eugene, OR 97401

www.wipfandstock.com

PAPERBACK ISBN: 978-1-6667-7001-8
HARDCOVER ISBN: 978-1-6667-7002-5
EBOOK ISBN: 978-1-6667-7003-2

Cataloging-in-Publication data:

Names: Elgvin, Torleif, author.

Title: My lips play flute for the highest : Jewish hymns and prayers before Jesus / Torleif Elgvin.

Description: Eugene, OR: Cascade Books, 2024. | Includes bibliographical references.

Identifiers: ISBN 978-1-6667-7001-8 (paperback). | ISBN 978-1-6667-7002-5 (hardcover). | ISBN 978-1-6667-7003-2 (ebook).

Subjects: LSCH: Prayer—Judaism. | Dead Sea Scrolls. | Qumran community. | Jews—History—586 B.C.–70 A.D. | Judaism—Early works to 1800.

Classification: BM487 E44 2024 (print). | BM487 (epub).

VERSION NUMBER 11/19/24

Contents

Figures

Acknowledgments

FOR TRANSLATION OF QUMRAN texts, I consulted Accordance; Vermes 1997; Wise, Abegg, and Cook 1996; García Martínez and Tigchelaar 1997, 1998. For the Thanksgiving Hymns, Schuller and Newsom 2012 was particularly helpful, I follow their line numbering of the columns. I am indebted to all of these, particularly to Vermes, but usually provide my own translation.

For the Old Testament Apocrypha, I consulted NRSV, the *New English Translation of the Septuagint* (NETS), and particularly *The Jerusalem Bible* (1966). For Jubilees, I consulted VanderKam 2020 and Charlesworth 1985. For the Psalms of Solomon and Joseph and Aseneth, I consulted Fink 2008 and the translations in Charlesworth 1985 and Wright 2007. For 1 Enoch, Nickelsburg 2001 was particularly helpful.

Often a poetic structure has been given priority over a literal rendering of the original text. The introductions to the apocrypha are indebted to *The SBL Study Bible*. Some of the introductions to Qumran texts are indebted to the *T. & T. Clark Companion to the Dead Sea Scrolls*. In biblical quotations I have provided my own translations. Thanks are due to Joseph D. Scales, who kindly read through the historical introductions and gave valuable feedback.

I am grateful to Jeremy Funk for his copyediting and to K. C. Hanson for his editing of the volume.

Glossary of Central Terms

Cairo Genizah — The archival room for used-up scrolls in the Cairo Karaite synagogue. The genizah contained remnants of thousands of manuscripts from medieval times. It was made known in the West by the scholar Solomon Schechter in 1896. The Karaites were a conservative Jewish movement that in the eighth century parted from the rabbinic stream, which was led by the head of the Jews in Mesopotamia, the exilarch.

Codex — Writing bound in the form of a book, in contrast to a scroll.

Essenes — Conservative Jewish movement in Judea, described by the first-century Jewish writers Philo and Josephus as well as some early Roman and Christian writers.

Hasmonean — From Simon, the last of the Maccabean brothers, who ruled Judea (142–34 BCE), this dynasty of priestly rulers was called the Hasmoneans, possibly after one of their ancestors. The Hasmonean period lasted until the Roman conquest in 63 BCE.

Midrash — Jewish exegesis of the Bible, and exegetical commentaries written within the rabbinic movement from the third century CE onwards.

Septuagint — The early Greek translation of the Hebrew Bible and the Old Testament Apocrypha. The various books of the Hebrew Bible were translated from the third century BCE until the late first century CE. The earliest preserved Septuagint codices are those known as Sinaiticus, Alexandrinus, and Vaticanus, from around 400 CE.

Introduction

What Can We Learn from Early Jewish Texts?

According to scholarly consensus, the latest book in the Old Testament was written around 160 BCE. John the Baptist and Jesus appeared on the scene in Judea and Galilee in 27 CE. Did the God of Israel go on vacation for two hundred years? What do we know about Jewish faith, hope, and literature in the centuries between 160 BCE and 27 CE?

This book tries to answer these questions by walking through Jewish texts from the second and first centuries BCE. Jewish literature blossomed in this period. We know scrolls that were on the shelves of the synagogue in Nazareth, we know others that Paul's rabbinic teacher in Jerusalem also knew, and we know books that New Testament writers knew but that did not enter Jewish or Christian Bibles. Some of the texts presented here were known and used only in restricted circles in Judea, while others represent common Jewish ideas in the realms of faith, hope, reflection, and biblical exegesis. These texts show us the heritage of Israelites we encounter in the New Testament; they were written as history moved toward what Paul calls "the fullness of time" (Gal 4:4).

Some Christian readers might brush aside Jewish texts from before Jesus, claiming that "the New Testament is sufficient for us—we do not need earlier texts that did not enter our canon." But the New Testament does not claim that the God's holy spirit had departed from Israel in the generations before the turn of the era. The texts presented here may reflect the presence of God among the people of Israel and give glimpses of how he led them through the changing eras of history. They show how different scribes and sages gave expression to their faith and hope, and to their struggle to understand the ways of God in times of suffering and trials.

The Significance of the Texts Today

I have gathered a large selection of poetic texts from Judean writers—prayers, psalms, and visionary texts. The nature of humanity has not changed much during two thousand years. Souls and hearts may resonate more easily with ancient prayers, psalms, and poetry than with catechisms and theological treatises. Readers might experience that these texts are durable: some may still be used in prayers to the Highest or to evoke a sense of awe.

Brief comments accompany each of the texts. For those who want to delve deeper into the books, milieus, and traditions behind these texts, more comprehensive introductions to each literary text follow in the last section of the book. There I also provide references to further study of relevant scholarly literature.

A Jewish reader would not ask about what would fall "between the two testaments of the Bible." He might ask about Judean traditions from late Second Temple times, from the period when the books of the Hebrew Bible were finalized, edited, and polished. What occupied the minds of Judean writers from the time of the Maccabees and until the Mishnah began to take shape after the Bar Kokhba revolt in the second century CE? *My Lips Play Flute for the Highest* will give some answers to this question, showing how Jews were praying and singing in those days.

Some Jewish readers might question why I draw lines to New Testament writings at all. In making these connections, I do not suggest any ecclesiastical victory for Christianity over Judaism or that Jewish hopes belong to the past. Rather, the lines between these Jewish texts and Christian ones might illustrate how the New Testament is a collection of Jewish writings from the first century and needs to be interpreted in the light of contemporary Jewish tradition and the Hebrew Bible.

In the light of contemporary texts from Judea, the teacher and prophet from Nazareth and his followers emerge as sons of Israel and children of their time. As one example, Jesus was not the first Jewish teacher portraying God as a loving Father. Was Jesus right in his claim of having a unique relation to the God of Israel? Were New Testament authors right when they confessed that he was the expected messiah? Here Jews and Christians have different answers. As a Christian scholar, I do not hide my own confession. However, the texts I bring forward from various depositories belong to a tradition that is common to Jews and Christians, from the time before the Temple was destroyed and the ways of synagogue and church would gradually part from each other. The texts belong to traditions that became formative for cultures around the world. From some of them there are lines of development to early Jewish mysticism.

The Depositories and Sources

Most of the texts in this book were found in the Judean Desert. The Dead Sea Scrolls preserve remnants of an ancient library belonging to the scribal center of a conservative Jewish group located at the northwestern edge of the Dead Sea. Here some ancient Essenes established a settlement close to Wadi Qumran, a center that was active from some time in the first century BCE and until 68 CE, when Roman soldiers laid Qumran desolate during their campaign to crush the great Jewish Revolt.

The Essenes were a traditionalist group led by learned priests who became opposed to the ruling Hasmonean elite during the time Judea was on its way to Jewish independence and parted from the Temple establishment around the mid-second century. Some of the scrolls suggest that an Essene subgroup gathered around a priest they later would call "the Teacher of Righteousness." He would teach his followers to read biblical texts as prophecies about their own group, the righteous remnant of Israel in the last days. There are parallels between this community and the Teacher's role and self-consciousness and what we later encounter with the appearance of Jesus and those following him.

Remnants of 950 scrolls were found in eleven of the many caves around Qumran, some so close to the settlement that they were part of the center's daily life.

We talk about *book scrolls*. The bound book, the *codex*, was hardly invented. Scrolls were made of papyrus from Egypt and from skins of sheep, goats, and cattle from Judea. Some of the scrolls unearthed here were produced through a remarkably advanced technology; some parchment scrolls from this time are of a quality not surpassed anywhere in the world. In the cave depositories, some of the rolls were stored vertically in jars originally produced to store ritually pure foodstuffs, often called "scroll jars." These scrolls were better preserved than their "cousins" lying on the cave floor, which gradually was covered with layers of soil and dung from bats and rats.

The scrolls were found in the caves around Qumran by Bedouin and archaeologists between 1947 and 1956. Some of the scrolls were completely or almost completely preserved. Most of them, however, survived only in smaller or larger fragments. The process of deciphering, interpreting, and publishing the texts lasted for decades. Since the early 2000s all the texts have been known. The process of interpreting the texts and drawing lines to other early Jewish and Hellenistic literature continues. Scholars continue to make new editions and "reconstruct scrolls"—i.e., placing the fragments in their original positions in the roll, thereby understanding more of the sequence of the fragments and the line of argument in the text. Some writings were preserved in more than one fragmentary copy, enabling restoration of original text through overlapping passages.

Large scrolls were found relatively well preserved in Cave 1 and Cave 11, natural caves in the cliffs at some distance north of the settlement. Here important scrolls were hidden before the Roman armies conquered Jericho and subsequently destroyed Qumran in June 68, during the third year of the First Jewish Revolt. Cave 4, at the outskirts of the settlement, probably served as a depository and literary archive for this scribal center. In this cave, fragmentary remnants of around six hundred scrolls were found worn and torn on the cave floor. With some compositions present in numerous copies in the caves, around five hundred literary texts may be identified among the Qumran scrolls.

The settlement at Qumran belonged to an elite, puritanical group within the Essene movement, whose members called themselves the "Union" (*Yahad*). More than 150 of the literary works identified among the scrolls bear characteristics of the Union—they assume and reflect its organizational pattern and hierarchic structure, its liturgies and puritanical way of life, its specific phraseology and scribal habits. The Qumran library also included writings from their "fathers," or books belonging to the wider Judean literary heritage. Some of these books were known from before—Sirach, Tobit, Jubilees, and 1 Enoch—early Jewish books later transmitted and copied in Christian circles and monasteries in other languages than the original Hebrew or Aramaic.

To provide a wider and more representative selection of Jewish texts from the second and first centuries BCE, this book includes several texts not found in the Qumran caves, texts from the Old Testament Apocrypha (or deuterocanonical books)—a group of texts included in early biblical codices from the fifth century onwards, books usually contained in Catholic and Orthodox Bibles but not in most Protestant versions of the Old Testament. From the apocrypha I have included texts from 1 and 2 Maccabees, Sirach, Tobit, Judith, the Wisdom of Solomon, and the Prayer of Manasseh.

Other early Jewish writings were loosely designated by biblical scholars Old Testament pseudepigrapha, a term chosen because several of these writings were published under the names of biblical sages (that is, pseudonymously), and they were published in scholarly collections of pseudepigrapha from the eighteenth century onwards. From these I have included texts from 1 Enoch and Jubilees (books esteemed as biblical in the Ethiopic Church), Enoch and the Giants, Joseph and Aseneth, Psalms of Solomon, and Testament of Levi.

The terms Old Testament Apocrypha and Old Testament Pseudepigrapha are hardly precise as literary categories ("apocryphal" means "hidden"). They designate relatively random collections of early Jewish writings that became popular in churches. Today we know that they are part of a flowering Jewish literary tradition from the late Second Temple period. The Dead Sea Scrolls gave scholars an unexpected window into this wider tradition.

The texts are translated close to the original Hebrew, Aramaic, Greek, and Ethiopic. A translation always includes a level of interpretation; this also goes for the texts included here. At times a poetic structure has been given priority over a literal rendering. In the process I consulted other published translations; see the references at the end of the book.

Torleif Elgvin
Oslo, February 2024

Fig. 1: The Great Isaiah Scroll, 1QIsa[a], photographed in 1948. The scroll was copied by two scribes of the Qumranite Union around 100 BCE. Copyright © Dr. John C. Trever. Digital image by James E. Trever.

Hymns of Praise

Praise to him who created the earth by his might

Hymn to the Creator, 11QPsalms[a] column 26

Great and holy is the Lord,
the most holy through all the ages!
At his fore marches majesty,
at his rear, the tumult of many waters.
Loving-kindness and truth surround his face,
truth, justice, and righteousness are the pedestal of his throne.

He divided light from darkness,
he established the dawn by the knowledge of his heart.
When all his angels saw it, they rejoiced in song,
for he showed them what they had not known.
He crowns the hills with fruit
and provides nourishment for all the living.

Praise to him who made the earth by his might,
who established the world by his wisdom
and stretched out the heavens by his understanding!
He brings forth [the winds] from his st[ores],
sending lightning and rain,
making vapors to rise from the ends of [the earth].
[. . .]

The largest preserved psalm scroll from Qumran was found by the Bedouin in Cave 11, three kilometers north of Qumran, in 1956. In addition to thirty-two psalms from the last third of the biblical Psalter, the preserved parts contained eight nonbiblical psalms, some of which were known from the Book of Sirach or some early Syriac Bibles. The scroll was intended for liturgical use, it was a songbook for the Qumran community. At least some of the nonbiblical psalms were composed before the rise of the Essene movement and may preserve hymns sung in the temple.

This hymn, not known previously, can be compared with biblical hymns. This hymn's newness appears in the naming of the attributes of God with their role in the act of creation and with God's heavenly entourage as a praising audience. Creation is not a one-time act, the creator cares for all living beings and provides nourishment for them.

As source texts the poet used scriptures such as Gen 1; Ps 33:6–7; Ps 103; Prov 3:19–20, 8:22–31; Deut 33:2; and Hab 3:3–4. He recast the biblical material into a new work, a poetic hymn to the creator.

The lower part of the scroll has decomposed, so we lack the end of the hymn. Square brackets in this and other texts indicate (tentative restoration of) lacunae in the scrolls and fragments, which had suffered extensive damage during their two-thousand-year sojourn in Judean Desert caves (small lacunae with obvious restorations are usually not specified).

On 11QPsalms[a], see pp. 164–67.

Heavenly singers, give him honor and praise
4Q403, Songs of the Sabbath Sacrifice frg. 1, 1:30–43

For the Master.
The song accompanying the Sabbath sacrifice on the seventh Sabbath,
sung on the sixteenth of the second month.

Praise to you, God the Most High,
exalted among all wise divine beings.
Let the holy among the godlike sanctify the king of glory,
the holy one who sanctifies all his holy ones.
You princes of praise among all the godlike,
praise the God of majestic praises.
For in the splendor of praises is the glory of his kingship.
therein are held the praises of all the godlike,
together with the splendor of his entire realm.

You godlike among the exalted in heaven,
exalt his exaltation on high,
his glorious divinity above the highest heavens.
He [is the God of gods] among the princes on high,
king of kings over all eternal councils.

By his wise will and through the words of his mouth
come into being all [the exalted godlike ones],

at the opening of his lips, all eternal spirits.
By his wise will, all his creatures in their undertakings.

Rejoice, you who exult in [knowing Him],
with a joyful song among the wondrous godlike.
Sing his praise with the tongue of all who sing about his wondrous knowledge,
with the mouth of all who sing [to him.
He] is the God of all who exult in everlasting knowledge,
the mighty judge over all perceptive spirits.

Divine beings, celebrate the king of majesty.
The godlike of knowledge sing his praise,
the spirits of righteousness celebrate his truth,
they seek acceptance of their knowledge by the judgments of his mouth,
of their jubilation when his mighty hand dispenses judgment.
Sing praises to the mighty God with an offering of princely spirit,
a song of divine joy and a jubilation among all the holy,
a wonderful song for eternal rejoicing.

The [foundations of the hol]y of holies shall partake in praise,
the pillars bearing the highest abode,
yea, all the corners of the temple's structure.
Sing to the God who is awesome in strength,
[all you wise spirits of light],
together laud the brilliant firmament that girds his holy temple.
Praise him, godlike spirits,
forever praise the firmament of the highest heaven,
all [its bea]ms and walls, all its structure and crafted design.

The Songs of the Sabbath Sacrifice were meant for recital and singing when the daily sacrifice was carried forth in the temple on the Sabbath. The conductor of the Levitical choir enjoyed the privilege of leading both singers on earth and angels in heaven. At times he calls on the pillars of the heavenly temple to resound in harmony with the earthly and heavenly singers—there is a spiritual union between the worshipers below and those performing before the heavenly throne. In the songs, the angels are called *'elim*, "godlike beings." They are not seen as on par with the God the Most High, the one addressed in their praises.

The Essene community saw itself as a spiritual temple, where praises and prayers would substitute for temple sacrifices. These songs were sung at the time of the two daily sacrifices—also on the Sabbath a blameless lamb was to be sacrificed in the morning and at sunset (Exod 29:38–43).

Praise and adoration permeate the songs, songs lauding the God "who is enthroned over the praises of Israel" (Ps 22:4). Priestly texts of the Torah know that God is enthroned in the Holy of Holies. Heaven and earth meet at the temple altars so that God can provide atonement for and be in communion with humans. And so that the angels in heaven can sing in union with the temple choir below.

On Songs of the Sabbath Sacrifice, see pp. 167–68.

My lips play flute after his guiding line

Community Rule, 1QS 10:8–18

His engraved precepts shall be on my tongue as long as I live,
as the fruit of praise and portion of my lips.
I will sing with knowledge;
all my music shall be for the glory of God.
The strings of my lyre sound for his holy order;
my lips play flute after his guiding line.

With the coming of day and night,
I will enter into the covenant of God.
With the departure of evening and morning,
I will recite his decrees.
In his laws I will place my boundary and never turn back.

I will declare his judgment concerning my sins,
my transgressions are before my eyes
as an engraved statute.
To God I say, "My righteousness,"
to the Most High, "You are my foundation,
fountain of knowledge, source of holiness,
the height of glory, the mighty eternal majesty."
What he teaches me, I will follow;
when he prescribes my way, I shall delight.

As soon as I stretch out my hand or my foot,
I will bless his name.
As soon as I go out or come in,
to sit down or rise up,
and while I recline on my couch,
I will cry out to him.

When in ranked array,
I will bless him with the offering of my lips,
and before I lift my hands to eat
of the pleasant fruits of the earth.
I will bless him for his wonderful deeds
at the beginning of fear and dread
and in the abode of distress and desolation.
I will meditate on his power
and lean on his mercies all day long.

I know that the judgment of all the living is in his hand,
and proclaim that all his deeds are truth.
I will praise him when distress is unleashed,
in his salvation I will rejoice.

I will pay to no man the reward of evil,
I will pursue him with goodness.
For judgment of all the living is with God,
it is he who will render to man his reward.

The Community Rule is the main catechism of the Qumran community. It is preserved in eleven shorter editions from Caves 4 and 5 and in a longer version from Cave 1, a beautifully inscribed "library copy" from around 100 BCE.

After nine columns of theological reflection, a covenant-renewal liturgy, and rules for the members, the scroll ends with a long composite prayer, also present in three of the Cave 4 copies. This psalm of confidence and the text on pp. 94–96 are excerpts from this long psalmic prayer text.

The Qumran movement may be the first group in Jewish history that prescribed daily individual prayer, as early as the second century BCE. The contents of 10:8–18 suggest that this psalm is closely related to the morning and evening prayers for the community member, liturgical prayers that would be directed to God in the second person.

On the Community Rule, see pp. 168–71.

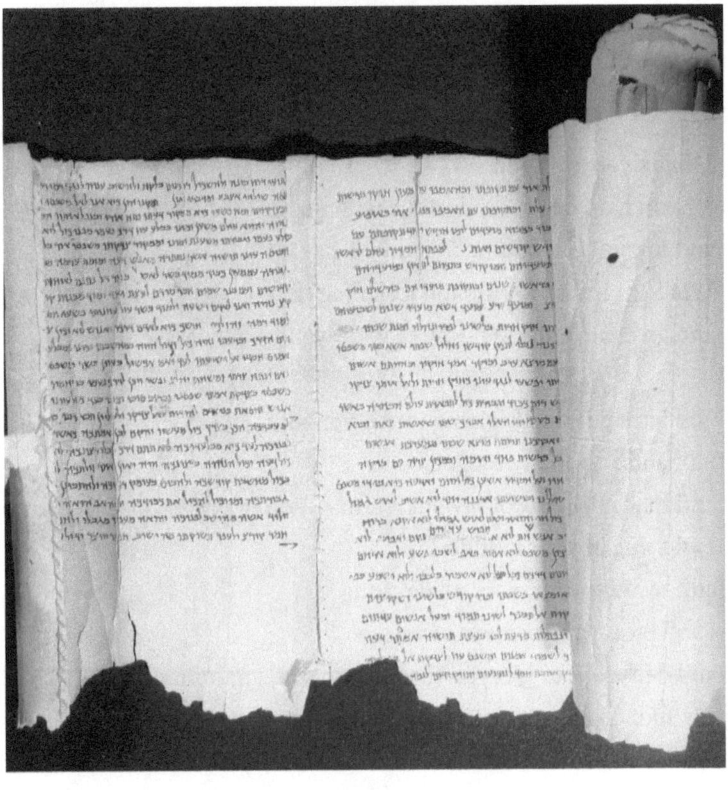

Fig. 2: The end of the Community Rule, with columns 10 and 11. Note the traces of sewing at the end that connected 1QS with its first appendix, 1QSa. Column 10 was a single sheet of parchment. Courtesy Shrine of the Book. Rule was attached. Photo: Moshe Kirschner, 1954. Courtesy of Israel Museum, Jerusalem, Shrine of the Book.

You enlighten me about your wondrous deeds

1QH[a] 19:6–17

I thank you, my God,
for you have dealt wonderfully with dust,
and mightily towards a creature of clay.
What am I, that you should teach me the counsel of your truth
and give me understanding of your wonderful works?

You have put thanksgiving into my mouth,
jubilation upon my tongue,
and made the flow of my lips a foundation of praise.
I will sing of your kindness
and recount your glory all day long.
I will bless your name at any time
and declare your glory in the midst of the sons of men.
My soul delights in your great goodness.

I know that your word is truth,
that righteousness is in your hand,
and all knowledge in your thoughts.
All power is in your might,
all glory is with you.
In your wrath are all chastisements,
but in your goodness is abundant forgiveness;

your mercy is for all the sons of your goodwill.
For you have made known to them
the secret counsel of your truth,
and taught them your wonderful mysteries.

For the sake of your glory you have purified man
from sin that he may be holy for you,
from all impure abomination and guilty wickedness,
so that he might be united with your true children
and partake in the lot of the holy angels,
so that bodies gnawed by worms may be raised from the dust
to the council of your truth,
so that a perverse spirit may be lifted to knowledge of you,
that he may stand before you
with the everlasting host and the eternal spirits,
so that he may be renewed together with all the living
and rejoice together with the men of knowledge.

THE MEMBERS OF THE Qumranite Union know that in themselves they are bound to impurity and iniquity, but God has made them his true children and sons of his goodwill, so that they may partake in the angelic praise of the Lord. The Hebrew phrase "sons of (your/his) goodwill" will recur in Luke's rendering of the song of the angels: ". . . and peace on earth among men of goodwill" (Luke 2:14). To the elect community of the end-time God has revealed the secret counsel of his truth. We find the same thoughts and ideas in the words of Paul in Eph 1:7–12.

On the Thanksgiving Hymns, see pp. 171–72.

Fig. 3: The Thanksgiving Hymns, artwork by Lika Tov

He circumcised the foreskin of their heart

4QBarkhi Nafshi, 4Q434 frg. 1:1–13

Bless my soul, the Lord,
for all his marvels forever.
Blessed be his name;
he delivered the soul of the poor.
He did not despise the humble
or overlook the misery of the deprived.

He has opened his eyes towards the distressed;
he has heard the cry of the fatherless;
he has turned his ears towards their crying.
He has been gracious to the humble in his great mercy;
he opened their eyes to see his ways
and their ears to hear his teaching.
He circumcised the foreskin of their heart;
he delivered them in his mercy;
he set their feet firm on the path.

In their many hardships he did not forsake them;
he did not hand them over to the violent,
nor did he judge them together with the wicked.
His anger was not enkindled against them;
he did not destroy them in his wrath.

While all his furious wrath was not growing weary,
he did not judge them in the fire of his zeal.
He judged them by his abundant mercies,
and sent grievous judgments only to test them.

In his abundant mercy he brought them back from among the nations,
and delivered them [from the hands of brutal] men.
He did not judge them amid the mass of nations,
and did not [abandon] them in the midst of the gentiles.
No, he hid them in [the palm of his hand,]
"He made dark places light before them;
he made rough paths into a plain" [Isa 42:16],
and revealed to them paths of peace and truth.

He has made their spirits by measure
and has established their words by weight,
and made them sing like flutes.
He gave them another heart,
so that they walk on the paths [of their Lord].
He brought them near to the path of his heart,
for they had risked their life's breath.
So he wove a protective hedge around them,
and commanded that no plague should smite them.
"His angels encamped around them" [Ps 34:7],
so that [Belia]l should not destroy them,
while the fire of his fury was kindled against their enemies.

THIS PSALM MAY HAVE been sung in the temple in Maccabean or pre-Maccabean times, recalling the early return from exile under Cyrus, and perhaps later returnees sieving into Judea in Persian and early Hellenistic times. The psalm's description of God's protection against violent enemies would be particularly relevant in Hasmonean times when the Hasmonean rulers steadily fought against the mighty Seleucid armies and neighboring nations.

The first part of the psalm praises God, who hears the cry of the poor and distressed and raises them from dust. Typical of this psalmic collection, body images are used to describe both the Lord above and humans below: "he opened their eyes to see his ways, / and their ears to hear his teaching. / He circumcized the foreskin of their heart / . . . / He gave them another heart / . . . / and brought them near to the path of his heart." The psalmist sings about God transforming the hearts of Israel with terms from Jeremiah and Ezekiel.

On the hymnic collection Barkhi Nafshi, see p. 172.

You love all the living

Wisdom of Solomon 11:20–26

People could fall at a single breath
when pursued by justice and scattered by the breath of your power.
You have arranged all things
by measure and number and weight.
For it is always in your power to show great strength;
who can withstand the might of your arm?
Before you the whole world is like a speck that tips the scales,
like a drop of morning dew that falls on the ground.

But you are merciful to all, for you can do all things.
You overlook people's sins, so that they may repent.
For you love all the living
and detest none of the things you have made,
for you would not have made anything if you had hated it.
How would anything endure if you had not willed it?
Or how would anything that was not called forth by you be preserved?
You spare all things, for they are yours, O Lord, you who love all the living.

THIS HYMNIC PASSAGE PRAISES the Creator of all living things, who loves all he has brought into being. Sinful man could be blown away by God's breath, but in God's mercy there is hope for forgiveness. The passage is included in the Wisdom of Solomon, belonging to the Old Testament Apocrypha.

On the Wisdom of Solomon, see pp. 173–75.

Prayers for Israel

Enoch's prayer

1 Enoch 84:2–6

Blessed are you, O Lord and King,
great and mighty in your majesty,
Lord of all created in heaven,
King of kings and God of all eternity.
Your power and reign abide forever,
your dominion to all generations.
The heavens are your throne forever,
all the earth is your footstool forever and ever.

For you have created and rule all things;
nothing is impossible for you.
Wisdom does not escape you;
it does not turn away from your throne or your presence.
All things you know, you see, and you hear;
nothing can be hidden from your eyes.

And now the angels of your heavens
are committing sin upon the earth,
and your wrath shall rest upon the flesh of men
until the great day of judgment.

And now, Lord and great King,
I make supplication, and request that you fulfill my prayer:

to leave me a remnant on the earth,
and not destroy all human flesh
and devastate the earth
with eternal destruction.
And now, my Lord, remove from the earth
the flesh that has aroused your wrath,
but sustain the seed of righteousness
as a seed-bearing plant to remain forever.
Do not hide your face from the prayer of your servant, O Lord.

According to Gen 5:24, "Enoch was walking with God, and then he was no more, for God took him"—so it is not strange that Enoch became a spiritual hero. Throughout the second century BCE, a collection of four books was formed, later called 1 Enoch or the book of Enoch. Learned and pious Judeans wrote down their visions of the heavenly spheres and what they expected to happen in the last days. They felt spiritually related to Enoch up in the highest—he had prayed for a righteous tribe of descendants—and published their books in his name.

The prayer put into Enoch's mouth presupposes that the flood was revealed to Enoch. (According to Genesis, Noah was his great-grandchild.) Enoch prays to God that he would make a new beginning for humankind, not least for the "seed of righteousness," "a seed-bearing plant to remain forever": the spiritual core in Israel that will lead the people to renewal.

This part of 1 Enoch (chapters 83–90, the Dream Visions) was written in the tumultuous years around 170 BCE, when sharp differences emerged between Jews open to Greek cultural influences and those who wanted to keep the traditions and commandments they had received from their fathers. On "the angels of heaven committing sin on the earth," see the commentary to the next text.

On 1 Enoch, see pp. 175–77.

Noah's prayer

Jubilees 10:3–6

Noah prayed to the Lord his God:
God, you who give breath of live to all living,
you showed me mercy;
you saved me and my sons from the flood,
that we should not perish
as you did to those meant for perdition.
Great is your grace toward me;
great is your mercy upon my soul.
Let your grace follow my sons;
do not let the evil spirits rule over them,
lest they destroy them from the earth.
Bless me and my sons;
let us grow and become numerous and fill the earth.

You know what your watchers, the fathers of these spirits,
have done during my lifetime—also these spirits who are alive today.
Shut them up and take them to the place of judgment.
Let them not cause corruption among the sons of your servant;
they are cruel and destined to cause destruction,
and you alone know how they will be punished.
Let them not rule over the spirits of men
nor have power over the sons of righteousness
from now on and forevermore.

The Book of Jubilees is a rewritten and expanded version of Genesis and Exodus that continues to grow throughout the first century BCE. The authors, who possibly were close to the Qumran movement, have a desire for spiritual renewal in the nation of Israel, something that would entail keeping the commandments according to their own understanding of torah, commandments, and purity. For them, the sages of Genesis would have followed the Torah of Moses and celebrated the Israelite festivals, even before the explicit revelation of these commandments.

According to the understanding of 1 Enoch and Jubilees, evil spirits are descendants of fallen angels, the "sons of God" who sinned before the flood and their offspring, the watchers or giants (Gen 6:1–4). Noah prays for protection against the evil spirits for all his descendants, all humankind, and particularly for "the children of the righteous," with the people of Israel and their pious ones in focus.

On Jubilees, see pp. 178–79.

Abraham's prayer

Jubilees 12:19–20

This night Abraham prayed:
God Most High, you alone are my God.
Everything is created by your hands,
and I have chosen you and your lordship.

Save me from the power of evil spirits,
those who rule over the thoughts of men,
so that they do not lead me away from you, my God!
Strengthen me and my descendants through all times,
so that we never go astray!

JUBILEES RECALLS THAT THE young Abraham believed in one God and renounced the idols. The book puts this prayer in Abraham's mouth when he is still in the land of Haran, before the Lord reveals himself to him (Gen 11:31). The prayer is timed to the "night of destiny"—that later would be called the Jewish New Year festival. God answers this prayer by revealing himself to Abraham (Gen 12:1–3).

On the story from Jubilees of Abraham's renouncing idols and believing in one God, see p. 180.

You renewed your covenant with us
1QFestival Prayers, 1Q34 frg. 3, 2:5–8

In the time of your goodwill
you chose for yourself a people.
You remembered your covenant,
you u[nited] them and set them apart
from all the peoples as holy to yourself.

And for them you renewed your covenant
through a glorious vision and the words of your holy [spirit],
by the works of your hands and the writing of your right hand,
that they might know the glorious instructions and the deeds that lead to eternity [. . .]
[You raised up] for them a faithful shepherd,
M[oses your servant, a ma]n of humility and gr[eat mer]cy.

A COLLECTIVE MESSIANISM IS reflected in a festival prayer that likely was part of the liturgy of the Union during the Feast of Weeks, with its covenant renewal. The Festival Prayers of the Union drew on liturgical traditions from Judea at large but were adapted and edited to fit the self-understanding of the community. This passage follows a reflection on man's trespassing the laws of God.

The liturgy recalls Israel's first shepherd, Moses—the Qumran movement saw themselves as walking in his footsteps. In the text, there is a seamless transition from the Sinai revelation and covenant to the Union's celebration and self-understanding. "You renewed your covenant" refers to both the covenant at Sinai and the yearly covenant renewal of the Union, which is the community of the new covenant. Just as in the Sinai event Israel was set apart from the nations, so the community is in the present set apart from ungodly Judea at large.

On Festival Prayers from Qumran, see pp. 180–81.

Look upon us in our trials

Words of the Luminaries, 4Q504 frgs. 1–2, 5:2—6:16

[They abandoned] the fount of living water
[. . .] and served a foreign god in their own land.
And their land, too, became a wasteland by the hand of their enemies.
For your wrath was poured out
and your burning anger was a zealous flame,
making the land a desert where no man could go or return.

Nevertheless, you did not reject the seed of Jacob
or cast Israel away to destruction,
breaking your covenant with them.
Surely you alone are the living God;
beside you is no other.
You remembered your covenant,
for you redeemed us in the sight of the nations,
you did not forsake us among the nations.

You showed mercy toward your people Israel
in all the lands to which you had exiled them.
You placed it on their hearts to turn to you,
to obey your voice
as you had commanded through your servant Moses.

For you have poured out your holy spirit upon us,
bringing your blessings to us.
You caused us to seek you in our time of tribulation,
that we might pour out a prayer
when your chastening was upon us.
We have gone through tribulations;
we have been stricken and tried by the fury of the oppressor.

Surely we have tired God with our iniquities,
wearyng the Rock through our sins.
Though we did not hearken to your commandments,
you steered us away from our own paths,
to walk on the right path and serve you. [. . .]

You have hurled all our transgressions away from us,
and purified us from our sins for your own sake.
Righteousness is yours alone, O Lord,
for it is you who have done all these things.
Now, on the day when our heart is humbled,
we expiate our iniquity and the iniquity of our fathers,
together with our unfaithfulness and rebellion.
We have not rejected your trials,
nor has our spirit loathed your chastisement,
so as to break our covenant with you,
despite all the distress of our soul
when you sent our enemies against us.

Surely it is you who have strengthened our hearts,
so that we may recount your mighty deeds
to everlasting generations.
O Lord, since you do wonders from eternity to eternity,

let your anger and wrath retreat from us.
Look upon our affliction, toil, and oppression,
and rescue your people Israel
from all the lands, near and far,
to which you have banished them,
each one who is inscribed in the Book of Life,
so that they can serve you and give thanks to you
[who rescued them] from all their oppressors.

THE QUMRANITES' DAILY LITURGY is preserved in Words of the Luminaries—prayers formulated for each day of the week, and likely inherited from their fathers or temple circles.

In this text there are no signs of the Hasmonean restoration and victories over their enemies. Israel is dispersed among the nations as a punishment for their sins, and most of the people reside in foreign lands. This penitential prayer asks God to turn the fortune of Israel and lead them back to their land. The praying community has experienced that God has shed his holy spirit upon them even in the land of their exile; he has inscribed in the Book of Life the names of those who turn to him.

On Words of the Luminaries, see pp. 182–83.

Do not turn us over to the nations

Psalms of Solomon 7

Do not dwell away from us, O God,
lest those who hate us without cause attack us.
For you have rejected them, O God;
do not let their feet trample your holy inheritance.

Discipline us as you wish,
but do not turn us over to the nations.
For if you should send the angel of death,
you would give him instructions to save us.
For you are kind;
you will not destroy us in your anger.
Since your name dwells among us, we will receive mercy,
and the nations will not triumph over us.

For you are our protection;
we will call on you, and you will hear us.
For you will have compassion on the people of Israel forever;
you will not reject them.
Always we carry your yoke;
you admonish us by the whip of your discipline.

You will direct us on the day we need your support,
showing mercy to the house of Jacob
on the day you have promised.

Psalms of Solomon is a collection of songs written in the Jerusalem area around the mid-first century BCE. The collection includes songs of praise, supplications, songs of penitence, prayers for Israel and the temple, and longings for the Davidic messiah. The authors are critical of the Hasmonean high priests and rulers until Judea comes under Roman rule in 63 BCE. The psalms see the Roman conquest as God's judgment on a disobedient nation. The authors stand at some distance from the temple establishment, still closely associated with the Hasmonean leaders. Members of early Pharisaic circles are among the plausible authors of these psalms.

This hymn may have been written before the Roman invasion, perhaps with the expanding empire on the horizon. It is a heartfelt supplication to the Lord of history that Judeans may still experience freedom and blessings. The hymn reminds God about his presence in the temple and promises to the nation.

On the Psalms of Solomon, see pp. 183 84.

You cast us out of the land you gave us

Psalms of Solomon 9

When Israel was taken into exile in a foreign land,
when they abandoned the Lord, their redeemer,
they were expelled from the inheritance
that the Lord had allotted them.
Israel was dispersed among all the nations
as God had told them,
so that your righteousness would be proven right
when you judged our lawless actions.

For you are a righteous judge over all the nations;
none who do evil can be hidden from your knowledge,
and you see the way of your righteous ones.
How could a man hide himself
from your eyes and your knowledge, O God?

We have freedom to choose, each his own way;
to do right and wrong is given into our hands.
In your righteousness you oversee the ways of men:
He who walks in truth saves up life for himself with the Lord;
he who walks in iniquity leads his life toward destruction;
the Lord judges a man and his house with righteousness.

To whom will you show mercy, O God,
except to those who call upon the Lord?
When we confess our sins
you will cleanse and restore our souls—
shame on us and on our faces
for all the evil we have done.
Who should you forgive, except those who have sinned?
You show mercy to the sinners who repent.

And now, you alone are God,
we are the people you chose to love.
Look upon us with compassion,
O God of Israel, for we are yours;
do not take your mercy away from us,
lest the nations attack us.
For you chose the seed of Abraham
above all the nations;
you put your name upon us, Lord;
it will shine upon us forever.
The covenant you made with our fathers reaches to us;
our hope is in you to whom our souls are looking.
May the mercy of the Lord
be upon the house of Israel forever.

For the author, Israel itself and its sins are to blame for its destiny, being dispersed among the nations after the collapse of the Judean state and the fall of the temple. However, God will pity his people when they turn to him.

This psalm reflects a Pharisaic view of man and his free will: man has freedom to choose, each his own way. It is in his own hands to do right or wrong, to turn to God or to live against his will. God knows who the righteous are—even though they too need God's mercy and forgiveness.

Save us from the Assyrians

Judith 9:7–12, 14

See the Assyrians, boasting in their army,
glorying in their horses and riders,
exulting in the strength of their infantry.
Trusting in shield and spear, in bow and sling,
they do not know that you are the Lord
who shatters the weapons of war;
yours alone is the title of Lord.

Break their violence with your might;
in your anger bring down their strength,
for they have resolved to pollute your holy precincts,
to defile the tabernacle, the resting place of your glorious name,
to break off the horns of your altar with the sword.
Observe their arrogance; send your fury on their heads.
Give needful courage to this widow's hand.
By the guile of my lips strike slave down with master,
and master with servant.
Break their pride by a woman's hand.

Your strength does not lie in numbers,
nor your might in powerful men.
You are the God of the humble, the help of the oppressed,

the support of the weak, the refuge of the forsaken,
the savior of the despairing.

Please, please, God of my father, God of the heritage of Israel,
master of heaven and earth, creator of the waters,
king of your whole creation—hear my prayer.
Demonstrate to every nation, every tribe,
that you are the Lord, God of all power and might,
the protector of Israel.

JUDITH IS A HORTATORY novel written around 100 BCE. The fictional setting is seventh-century Judah under attack by the Assyrian army, where Judith, a female hero, rises as the one who saves her city. In this prayer, Judith prays to God for the strength she needs to accomplish her plan—to seduce the enemy commander and kill him. The scene of Judith beheading Holofernes, the enemy commander, became a common motif in Christian art.

On the book of Judith, see pp. 184–85.

Gather your dispersed people

2 Maccabees 1:24–29

O Lord God, creator of all things—
dreadful, strong, just, and merciful—
the only king and benefactor, the only provider,
who alone are just, almighty and everlasting;
the deliverer of Israel from every evil,
who made our fathers your chosen ones and sanctified them:

Accept this sacrifice on behalf of all your people Israel;
protect your heritage and consecrate it.
Bring together those of us who are dispersed;
set free those in slavery among the gentiles;
look favorably on those held in contempt or abhorrence;
let the gentiles know that you are our God.
Punish those who oppress us and affront us by their insolence,
and plant your people in your holy place, as Moses promised.

In the first chapter of 2 Maccabees, an editor included a fictional account of the death of Antiochus Epiphanes, followed by the preparation for the purification of the temple. As the Maccabees prepare for the rededication of the Temple, they "remember" and repeat this prayer of Nehemiah, from when he offered sacrifice in the temple at the Festival of Booths, and God's fire miraculously ignited the firewood and the offering.

On 2 Maccabees, see pp. 185–90.

Not by force of arms

2 Maccabees 15:21–24

Judah the Maccabee, observing the masses confronting him, the glittering array of armor and the savagery of the war elephants, raised his hands to heaven and called on the Lord who works wonders, for he knew that it is not by force of arms, but as the Lord decides, that victory is granted by him to those who deserve it. He called upon the Lord in these words:

O Master, you sent your angel in the time of King Hezekiah of Judea,
and he destroyed no less than one hundred and eighty-five thousand
of Sennacherib's army.
So now, Sovereign of heaven,
send a good angel before us to spread terror and trembling.
By the might of your arm,
may those who speak blasphemous words
against your holy people be struck down.

We find this prayer in the last chapter of 2 Maccabees. The Seleucids are still controlling Jerusalem, and their commander Nicanor marches to Samaria to confront Judah the Maccabee and his forces in battle. Judah then turns to God for help against the powerful enemy army, before leading his forces to battle while they are praying in their hearts. After a smashing victory, they march to Jerusalem to celebrate their triumph, and they introduce the "Day of Nicanor" into the festival calendar on the day before Purim.

Prayers for Zion

Soon after King David conquered the fortress of Zion around 1000 BCE, Israelite faith came to focus on Jerusalem. The temple became the center of the Judahite nation and cult and played an essential role in the coronation of the kings of the Davidic line. The city around the temple was soon called Zion. In times of distress God could address the inhabitants as "(my) daughter Zion." The fall of the temple and the city by the hand of Nebuchadnezzar in 587 was the nation's largest trauma in the millennium before the turn of the era.

After seventy years and the return of a small part of the exiled people, the temple was built anew in the years 520–515. According to Ezra 3:12, the Second Temple looked small and insignificant compared to its predecessor, and hardly matched prophecies about a glorious future for Zion. Jerusalem nevertheless remained the center of the small province of Judah, which was subordinate to the Persian and then the Hellenistic Empire. The site of the Persian provincial government and the province's administrative center was the luxurious settlement at Ramat Rachel, four kilometers to the south.

According to archaeologists, Judea and Jerusalem remained small and insignificant until the second century BCE. During the Persian period (540–332 BCE), Judea grew from circa three thousand to around ten thousand inhabitants, and Jerusalem slowly reached five hundred, more a temple village than a temple city. During the third-century wars between the Ptolemies of Egypt and the Seleucids of Syria, Jerusalem was ravaged at least once. With the Seleucid takeover in 198, Jerusalem and Garizim of the Samaritans received privileges as temple towns. Thus, the high priest, Simon II, was allowed to implement large renovations: "He repaired the sanctuary and fortified the temple. He laid the foundations for the high double walls for the temple enclosure. He had a huge water cistern dug . . . and fortified the city against siege" (Sir 50:1–4).

There was still a mismatch between biblical promises about a glorious restoration and daily reality in Second Temple–period Judea. Nevertheless, the nation looked forward to a better future that their bards described in golden colors, in songs addressing God or the city of Zion: the people will be renewed and be governed by spirit-filled leaders. Even the surrounding nations will sense that the God of Israel is their creator and make pilgrimages to Zion. Few of these songs, however, dared to imagine a new Israelite state ruled by a king from David's line. These early songs of Zion would centuries later be followed by others that made their way into synagogue liturgy.

Later, in the Gospels, we hear about "all those looking for the redemption of Jerusalem" (Luke 2:38). The sacrificial ministry of the temple was less important for the early Jesus movement than it was for other Judean groups. But while the temple was still standing, Jerusalem remained the place of the "mother church." It was from there the teaching of God and his messiah spread across the land and extended beyond its borders. According to the church historian Eusebius, the Hebrew mother church remained in Zion up until the Bar Kokhba revolt (132–136 CE). The book of Revelation concludes by offering the hope of a new creation, with a description of the new Jerusalem—a city without a temple but clothed in the glory of God.

A new time of humiliation for Judea and Jerusalem came with the blasphemous king of Antioch, Antiochus Epiphanes (175–64). During his campaigns against Egypt, he ravaged Jerusalem and robbed the temple of its treasures. His desecration of the temple and his outlawing Jewish customs led to the Maccabean Revolt, which in time would lead to an exponential growth of Judea and a full-blown Judean state under Hasmonean priestly rulers (for more about the Hasmonean restoration, see pp. 202–6).

Let Zion be filled with songs of praise

Sirach 36:13–19

Gather all the tribes of Jacob,
and give them an inheritance, as from the beginning!
Have mercy, O Lord, on the people called by your name,
on Israel, whom you named your firstborn!

Have pity on the city of your sanctuary,
Jerusalem, the place of your dwelling!
Fill Zion with your majesty,
and your temple with your glory!

Bear witness to those whom you created in the beginning,
and fulfill the prophecies spoken in your name!
Reward those who wait for you;
let your prophets be found trustworthy!

Hear, O Lord, the prayer of your servants,
according to your goodwill toward your people,
so that all who live on the earth will know
that you are Lord, the God of the ages.

The author of the book of Sirach, Yeshua ben Sira (Greek: Jesus son of Sirach), led a school in Jerusalem in the 190s BCE (Sir 51:23). In his instructional book he included psalms and hymns, some of them likely authored by himself.

SIR 36:1–12 (THE VERSES preceding this psalm) is a petition for protection against Israel's enemies, asking God to reveal himself with signs and wonders and to defeat violent adversaries—a prayer reflecting the recent misfortune of Jerusalem. The prayer against enemies is followed by this prayer for Zion, where the city more than the temple is in focus. The singer sees that most of the nation resides in the diaspora. He prays for the fulfilment of biblical prophecies, the ingathering of the exiles, and renewed glory for the city of the temple, the sanctuary where God dwells with his divine presence.

On Sirach, see pp. 190–91.

The towers of Jerusalem shall be built of gold

Tobit 13:9–17

Jerusalem, Holy City,
God scourged you for your handiwork,
yet still will take pity on the sons of the upright.
Zion, thank the Lord as he deserves,
bless the king of ages and pray,
that your temple may be rebuilt with joy,
that within you he may comfort
those who have been dispersed,
that within you he may love
all those who have been distressed,
for all generations to come.

A bright light shall shine
over all the regions of the land.
Nations shall come from far away,
from all the ends of the earth,
to dwell close to the holy name of the Lord God,
with gifts in their hands for the King of heaven.
Within you, generation after generation
shall proclaim their joy,
and the name of the chosen city shall endure
through generations to come.

Cursed be any who affront you,
cursed be any who destroy you,
who throw down your walls,
raze your towers and burn your houses!
Blessed forever be all who build you!
Then you will exult and rejoice
over the sons of the upright,
for they will all have been gathered in
and will bless the Lord of the ages.

Happy are those who love you;
happy those who rejoice over your peace;
happy those who mourned over your punishment!
For they will soon rejoice within you,
witnessing how you will be blessed in days to come.

My soul blesses the Lord, the great King,
because Jerusalem shall be built anew
and his house forever and ever.
What bliss if one of my blood is left
to see your glory and praise the King of heaven!

The gates of Jerusalem shall be built
of sapphire and emerald,
all your walls of precious stone.
The towers of Jerusalem shall be built of gold,
their battlements of pure gold.
The streets of Jerusalem shall be paved
with ruby and stones from Ophir;
the gates of Jerusalem will resound with songs of exultation,
all her families will say,

"Hallelujah! Blessed be the God of Israel."
Within you they will bless his holy name forever and ever.

This ode to Zion, probably written in the early second century, appears toward the end of the apocryphal book of Tobit, a short story written either in Judea or the Eastern diaspora around 200 BCE. A hymn of praise was editorially put into the mouth of the elderly Tobit (13:1–8), ending with the words, "Let all men speak of his majesty, and acknowledge him in Jerusalem." With the song fading out with praises being sung in Jerusalem, a second editor found it pertinent to add this psalm of Zion, before the story continues with Tobit's death and last exhortation to his son Tobias (chapter 14).

The hymn addresses Zion in the second person, a psalmic literary form breaking through at this time, likely inspired by Deutero-Isaianic oracles addressed to Zion (Isa 49:14–26; 51:17–23; 52:1–2; 54).

Judea had witnessed generations of war between the Seleucids of Syria and Ptolemies of Egypt. At least once Jerusalem had been ravaged. In Ben Sira's own time, the Syrian king Antiochus III conquered Judea, gave financial incentives to the temple and the temple city, and stimulated the high priest Simon II to renovate the temple. There are no signs of these for Zion better days in the psalm—nor of the Maccabean restoration—so it may have been written before the Syrian conquest in 198 BCE. Judea remained a small and poor province centered around the temple, Jerusalem hardly having more than one thousand inhabitants. The glory promised by prophetic foresayings seemed far away.

It is in fresh memory that Jerusalem had been humbled with walls torn down during the third-century wars (cf. Dan 11:16, 20). The author looks forward to a glorious restoration of the small postexilic temple and the town around it, opening for the pilgrimage of the nations to Zion, as promised in Isa 2 and Zech 14. The hope of rebuilding Jerusalem is weaved into a description of Jerusalem of the end-time, for which one can compare the description in Rev 21.

On Tobit, see pp. 192–93.

Zion shall be honored all over the earth

11QPsalms[a] Zion, column 22

I will remember you, Zion, for a blessing;
with all my might do I love you.
May your memory be blessed forever!
Great is your hope, Zion;
the peace and salvation you await shall come.
Generation after generation shall dwell in you,
and generations of the pious be your ornament.
They who desire the day of your salvation
shall rejoice in the greatness of your glory.
At your glorious bosom they will suckle;
in your beautiful streets they will rattle their bangles.

You shall remember the pious deeds of your prophets,
and glorify yourself in the deeds of your pious ones.
Purge wrongdoing from your midst;
may lying and iniquity be cut off from you.
Your children shall rejoice within you;
your loved ones shall be joined to you.
How much they have hoped in your salvation;
how much your perfect ones have mourned for you!
Your hope, Zion, shall not perish;
your expectation will not be forgotten.

Is there a righteous man who has perished?
Is there a man who has escaped his iniquity?
Man is tested according to his way,
each one repaid according to his deeds.

Your oppressors shall be cut off from around you, Zion;
all who hate you shall be dispersed.
Praise that will please you, O Zion,
shall rise all over the world.
Time and again I will remember you for a blessing;
I will bless you with all my heart.
You shall attain to eternal righteousness,
and shall receive blessings from the noble.

Take to heart the vision that speaks of you,
the dreams given to prophets about you.
Zion, be exalted and increase;
give praise to the Most High, your redeemer!
May my soul rejoice in your glory!

A Zion-centered eschatology permeates one of the nonbiblical psalms in 11QPs[a]Zion, the Great Psalm Scroll from Qumran Cave 11. As in Tob 13, here Zion is addressed in the second person. Neither the temple nor the eschatological high priest is specifically mentioned.

There is still mourning for Zion. The pious are waiting for its restoration and glory, which will be seen and praised by all the nations. The psalm was likely written before the Hasmonean renovations of the Temple Mount and the building activities in Jerusalem, possibly even before the high priest Simon II's restoration of the Temple Mount in the 190s.

The Lord gathers his children from east and west

Psalms of Solomon 11

Sound in Zion the trumpet of the sanctuary;
announce in Jerusalem the voice of one bringing good news,
for God has watched over Israel and been merciful to them.

Stand on a high place, Jerusalem,
and look at your children,
coming from the east and the west,
assembled together by the Lord.
From the north they come in the joy of their God,
from distant islands God has gathered them.

He flattened high mountains into level ground for them;
the hills fled at their coming.
The forests shaded them as they passed by;
God made every fragrant tree to grow for them,
so that Israel may proceed
under the supervision of the glory of their God.

Jerusalem, put on the clothes of your glory,
prepare the robe of your holiness,
for God has spoken well of Israel forevermore.

May the Lord fulfil his promises about Israel and Jerusalem,
may the Lord raise up Israel by his glorious name!
May the mercy of the Lord be upon Israel forever!

THIS HYMN HERALDS JERUSALEM and the temple and sees crowds of Israelites returning from the diaspora to the land. The song draws on prophetic passages such as those in Isa 40–55. The hymn may be inspired by the influx of Jewish immigrants from the Eastern diaspora to the growing Hasmonean state in the late second and early first centuries.

For more on this psalm, see p. 194.

Psalms of Confidence

You give nourishment to all the living

Psalms of Solomon 5

My Lord and God, with joy will I praise your name
among those who know your righteous decisions.
For you are good and merciful,
the refuge of the poor;
do not turn away when I cry out to you.

No one takes booty from a strong man,
so who can take anything from all you have created
unless you give it for free?
A man and his destiny are on the scales before you;
we cannot add anything to the lot you have decreed.

When we are persecuted, we call on you for help;
you will not turn away from our petition,
for you are our God.
Do not lay your hand heavily on us
lest we sin under duress.
Even if you turn away from us,
we will not stay away, but turn to you.

For if I am hungry, I will cry out to you, my God,
and you will provide.

You feed the birds and the fish,
you send rain in the wilderness so that the grass will sprout,
to provide pasture in the wasteland for all the living.
If they are hungry, they will lift up their voice to you.

You feed kings and rulers and nations, O God,
and who is the hope of the poor and deprived, if not you, Lord?
And you will listen, for who is good and kind but you,
making the humble rejoice when you open your hand in mercy?
Alms from men may be meager and come late,
rarely are they given anew without a grudge.
What you give is abundantly good and rich;
he who hopes in you will not be lacking:
you pour out your goodness to all the world.

Blessed is he who receives from God what he needs;
he who has an excess of riches will fall into sin.
True blessing from the Lord
is moderate wealth and life in righteousness;
those who fear the Lord will be satisfied with good things.

In your kingship you show mercy to Israel.
Praise to the glory of God, for he is our king.

In this psalm there are elements of different genres: hymn, lament, and psalm of confidence. The poet belongs to the common people of the land. He knows poverty, need, and tribulation, and does not always experience God's presence and support. But he will not give up his faith in the Creator, the Lord of all. As God provides for all living things and the creatures of the land, he will care for the low and humble when they cry out to him. In his mercy he will look upon the people of Israel and those who fear the Lord.

I fell asleep and came close to dying

Psalms of Solomon 16

When my soul slumbered away from the Lord,
I sank into sleep for a while, far from God.
My soul was poured out toward death,
with sinners I came close to the gates of Hades.
My soul was drawn away from the God of Israel,
but the Lord came to my aid with his everlasting mercy.
He jabbed me as with a horse spur;
my protector and savior came to my rescue.

I give thanks to you, my God,
who came to my aid and saved me;
you did not count me with sinners destined for destruction.
Do not take your mercy away from me, O God;
let my heart remember you until I die.

Restrain me, O God, from intentional sin,
from any evil woman who seduces the foolish.
May the beauty of an indecent woman not deceive me,
or a sly sinner bringing me down.

Direct the work of my hands before you;
protect my steps so that I remember you.

Guard my tongue and lips to say words of truth;
put anger and fierce rage far from me.
In tribulations, keep grumbling and discouragement far from me.
If I sin, discipline me so that I return to you.

Support my soul with approval and happiness;
when you strengthen my soul, I will be satisfied with what you give.
For if you do not give strength,
how can the poor one endure discipline?
When a man is tried by mortal weakness,
your testing is in his flesh, in poverty and pain.
When the righteous endures all these things,
he will receive mercy from the Lord.

THE PSALM RECALLS THAT God tests and disciplines those who fear him, to lead them on the right path. Poverty and tribulation are interpreted as God's discipline or punishment. The third stanza shows that the psalm is put in the mouth of male singers—such skepticism about the indecent woman has roots in Proverbs. The psalm reflects personal life experience but is generally formulated so that it can constantly be used by other Judeans who turn to God.

Blessed is the man who has a pure heart

4Q525 Wisdom Text with Beatitudes frg. 1:1–3, frg. 2 2:1–7

[These are the words the teacher spo]ke with the wisdom God gave him,
[for his students to kno]w wisdom and discipline,
to increase their kn[owledge and grow] in understanding.

[Blessed is the man who has] a pure heart
and does not slander with his tongue.
Blessed are those who adhere to her statutes
and do not hold to the ways of iniquity.
Blessed are those who rejoice in her,
and do not burst forth in ways of folly.
Blessed are those who seek her with pure hands,
and do not pursue her with a treacherous heart.
Blessed is the man who has attained Wisdom
and walks in the torah of the Most High.
He directs his heart to her ways,
restrains himself by her corrections,
and takes delight in her chastisements.

He does not forsake her in the face of his trials,
nor will he abandon her in time of strain.
He will not forget her on the day of fear,

and will not despise her when his soul is afflicted.
For he will always meditate on her,
in times of distress he will ponder on her [ways . . .]
[He will place her] before his eyes
so as not to walk in the ways of [folly].

THIS SAPIENTIAL SCROLL CONTAINS a sequence of beatitudes, similar in style both to Psalm 1 and to Jesus' words in the Sermon on the Mount (Matt 5:3–10). He who fears the Lord will meditate on Wisdom from above. In this text, Lady Wisdom is equated with the torah of the Most High, God's teaching and guidance.

On early Jewish beatitudes, see pp. 194–95.

Blessed is he who calls on the name of the Lord

Psalms of Solomon 6

Blessed is the man who is ready to call on the name of the Lord.
When they remember the name of the Lord, they will be saved.
His ways are directed by the Lord;
the works of his hands are guarded by the Lord his God.

His soul will not be disturbed when nightmares come upon him;
he will not be frightened when crossing tumultuous rivers.
He rises from his sleep and blesses the name of the Lord;
when his heart is strong he sings out to the name of his God.
He prays to the Lord for everyone in his household;
the Lord will hear the prayers of all who fear him.

The Lord will fulfil every request from the soul that hopes in him.
Praised to the Lord, who shows mercy to those who truly love him!

The psalm draws on texts such as Pss 1 and 37; Isa 43:2; and Deut 6:7. It opens with a beatitude and is permeated by trust in the Lord and confidence in God's safeguarding the righteous one. Compared to texts from the Qumran community one here notes a more optimistic anthropology: sinful man is not an existential problem for this singer.

I called on my Father and he saved me from death

Sirach 51:1–12

I will give thanks to you, Lord and King,
and praise you, God my Savior.
I give thanks to your name,
for you have been my protector and helper
and have delivered my body from destruction,
from the snare of the lying tongue,
from lips that fabricate falsehood.

In the face of my adversaries
you have been my helper and delivered me
—in the greatness of your mercy and your name—
from the fangs of those who would devour me,
from the hand of those seeking my life,
from the many troubles I have endured,
from choking fire on every side,
from the heart of a fire I had not kindled,
from deep in the belly of Hades,
from the unclean tongue and the lying word,
the perjured tongue slandering me to the king.

My soul has been close to death;
my life had gone down to the brink of Hades.

They surrounded me on every side;
there was no one to support me,
I looked for someone to help,
and no one was there.

Then I remembered your mercy, Lord,
your deeds from earliest times:
how you deliver those who wait for you patiently,
and save them from the hand of their enemies.
I sent up my plea from the earth;
I begged to be delivered from death,
I cried out, "Lord, you are my Father,
do not forsake me in the days of trouble,
when there is no help against the proud.
I will praise your name unceasingly,
and sing hymns of thanksgiving."

And my plea was heard,
for you saved me from destruction,
you delivered me from that time of evil.
For all this I will thank you and praise you;
I will bless the name of the Lord.

In the Bible, God may be portrayed as the father of the nation of Israel (Exod 4:23; Hos 11:1–4) or as the father of the son of David sitting on the throne in Jerusalem (1 Sam 7:14; Ps 2:7). More commonly, God is likened to a loving and caring mother. Sirach 51 is the earliest text where an individual Israelite turns to God as a caring father. Addressing God with the words "Lord, you are my Father," the psalmist quotes from the royal Psalm 89 (v. 27): the closeness to God that has been the prerogative of the Davidic king is now "democratized" to be used by common Israelites in their prayers.

Longing for God

You are Father for the orphan

Joseph and Aseneth 12:1—13:15

Aseneth the Egyptian opened her mouth to God:
O Lord, God of the ages,
who created and gave breath to all . . .
With you I take shelter, Lord;
to you I cry out,
to you I bring my supplication,
to you I confess my sins,
to you I reveal my iniquity.

Spare me, Lord,
for I have sinned much before you;
I behaved godlessly and said abominable things.
My mouth is defiled by sacrifices to idols
and the altars of the Egyptians gods.
I have sinned, Lord;
before you I sinned much in ignorance,
worshiping dead and dumb idols.

And now I am not worthy to open my mouth to you, Lord.
I, Aseneth, daughter of Pentephres the priest,
virgin and queen—
once I was prospering in riches beyond all people,

proud and arrogant;
now I am an orphan, desolate, and abandoned by all.
With you I take shelter, Lord,
to you I bring my supplication,
to you I cry out;
save me from those who persecute me.

As a small and fearful child flees to her father,
who, stretching out his hands and lifting her up,
brings her close and puts his arms around her,
and as the child clasps her hands around his neck,
regaining her breath after fear,
and rests at her father's breast,
so that the father comes to smile at the child's confusion—
so you too, Lord, stretch out your hands to me
as a loving father, and lift me up.

The wild old lion persecutes me;
he is the chief of the gods of the Egyptians:
his children are the gods, the idols of the heathen.
I have come to hate them;
they belong to the lion's den.
I have thrown them all away and destroyed them.
The roaring lion persecutes me;
Lord, rescue me from his hands,
deliver me from his fangs,
lest he carry me off as his booty, tear me up,
and throw me into the flames;
lest the fire cast me into the hurricane,
and the hurricane wrap me up in darkness
and cast me into the depths of the sea;

lest the big sea monster swallow me,
so that I am destroyed forever and ever.

Rescue me, Lord, before all this comes upon me;
rescue me, Lord, for I am desolate.
My father and mother disowned me and said,
“Aseneth is not our daughter,”
since I destroyed their gods and ground them to pieces,
because I had come to hate them.

Now I am a desolate orphan;
I have no other hope save in you, Lord,
no other refuge except your mercy, Lord.
For you are a father of orphans,
a protector of the persecuted,
a helper of the afflicted.

Have mercy upon me, Lord,
and protect me, a virgin, abandoned and alone;
for you, Lord, are a sweet and gentle father.
What father is as sweet as you, Lord;
who is so quick in mercy as you;
who is as long-suffering toward our sins as you?

Corruptible and transient are the gifts
my father Pentephres gave me as an inheritance,
but the gifts of your inheritance, Lord,
are incorruptible and eternal.

13:1 See my humiliation, Lord,
and have mercy upon me.

Look at me, the orphan,
and have compassion on me.
For I have fled from everything
and taken shelter with you, Lord.
See, I left behind all the good things of the earth
and took shelter with you, Lord.

In sackcloth and ashes I stand before you:
naked and without parents.
I put aside my royal robe,
interwoven with purple and gold,
and dressed myself in a black tunic.
I threw away my golden girdle
and girded a rope and sackcloth around myself.
My tiara and my diadem I threw off my head
and sprinkled ashes upon it instead.
The floor of my chamber, paved with a colored mosaic,
once anointed with myrrh and dazzling linen carpets,
is now smeared with ashes and sprinkled with my tears . . .
Seven days and seven nights I have fasted;
I have eaten no bread and drunk no water;
my mouth has become dry as a drum—
my tongue is like a horn and my lips like a potsherd . . .
my strength has left me entirely.

See, all the gods whom I worshiped in ignorance,
now I see they are only dumb and dead idols.
I caused them to be trampled down by men;
thieves snatched those of silver and gold.

With you I have taken shelter, O Lord my God.
Pardon me, for I sinned against you in ignorance;

this virgin spoke blasphemous words against my lord Joseph.
I did not know that he is your son;
people told me he was a shepherd's son from Canaan.
Poor me, I believed them and fell into error;
I despised him and spoke wicked words about him,
not knowing that he is your son.

For who among men has such a beauty,
such wisdom and virtue and strength?
Lord, I commit him to you,
for I love him more than I love myself.
Preserve him by your wisdom and grace.
Lord, let me be his maidservant and slave,
I will make his bed and wash his feet;
I will wait for him and be his maidservant forever and ever.

THE BIBLE RECORDS THAT Pharaoh gave Aseneth to Joseph as a wife. She was a priest's daughter from the temple city of On (Gen 41:45). This short note inspired a Judean author, probably living in Egypt in the second century BCE, to write the beautiful novel called Joseph and Aseneth.

The book proclaims the God of Israel as the only living God. It follows Aseneth's path from worshiping the Egyptian idols to recognizing Joseph's faith as the only true way. In a long penitential prayer, Aseneth confesses her idol worship as sin. She turns to God as a loving father and asks him to receive her as he has received Joseph as his son.

On Joseph and Aseneth, see pp. 196–98.

You receive the penitent one
Prayer of Manasseh

Lord Almighty, God of our fathers Abraham, Isaac and Jacob,
and of their righteous offspring,
you who made heaven and earth with all the world,
who shackled the sea by your word of command,
who shut up the deep and sealed it with your awesome and glorious name:

All things shudder and tremble before you;
your great glory cannot be borne;
nobody can stand before your threatening wrath against sinners.
Yet the mercy you have promised cannot be measured,
for you are the Lord Most High,
compassionate, slow to anger, and abounding in mercy;
you repent at the judgment you had decreed for men.

You are God of the righteous, those who do not need to repent,
such as Abraham, Isaac, and Jacob, who had not sinned against you;
but you have appointed repentance for me, the sinner.
The sins I have committed are more in number than the sand of the sea;
my transgressions multiplied, Lord; yes, they multiplied.
I am not worthy to raise my eyes and look up to heaven,

because of all my iniquities.
Bent down I am by iron fetters; my sins turn me away.
I find no relief, for I provoked your anger;
what is evil in your sight I have done:
I set up blasphemous idols and multiplied objects of wrath.

And now I bend the knee of my heart,
begging for kindness from you.
I have sinned, Lord, I have sinned;
my lawless acts I know.
I plead and beg you, forgive me, Lord, forgive me!
When you annihilate my lawless acts, do not destroy me.
Do not be angry with me forever or retain evil for me;
do not condemn me to the depths of the earth.

For you, Lord, are the God of those who repent;
show your goodness also toward me,
for, unworthy as I am, you will save me in your great mercy.
Then, I will praise you all the days of my life,
for all the host of heaven sings your praise,
and yours is the glory forever. Amen.

The Bible tells us that Manasseh was the most ungodly of the kings in Jerusalem (2 Kgs 21:1–18). However, Chronicles provides information not contained in 2 Kings: before he died, Manasseh made penitence, prayed to God for mercy, and received clemency (2 Chr 33:1–20).

An early Judean writer asked himself what kind of prayer the king might have prayed, and wrote this penitential prayer in his name—filling out information "lacking" in the biblical text. This text was composed sometime around the turn of the era.

The prayer expresses that it is never too late or impossible for a sinner to repent, turn to God, and receive forgiveness. When talking about "the righteous, those who do not need to repent," this text deviates from the view of man we encounter in Essene psalms and prayers. The singers of the Qumranite Union knew that all men are born unclean and turn away from God, without any hope for mercy in themselves (see the texts on pp. 12–13, 87–96).

On the Prayer of Manasseh, see pp. 198–99.

Burning for God's Wisdom

Sirach 51:13–19/11QPsalms[a] 21:11–17

When I was still young and had not yet strayed or sought her,
she came to me in her beauty,
and right to the end I will seek her.
Even when the blossoms fade, the grapes still rejoice the heart.

My foot trod in the plain field,
for from my youth have I known her closely.
Scarcely bending my ear, I found much instruction.
She became a wet nurse to me; to my teacher I pay respect.

I pondered; I wanted to play.
I desired the good things and did not let anything distract me.
I was on fire with her and would not turn back.
I was stirred up by her and did not stray from her heights.
My hand opened [her mountain of myrrh]:
I gazed on her nakedness,
I purified my hand toward [her hill of frankincense].

In the last chapter of his book, Ben Sira includes a song about his intense longing for "Lady Wisdom," the God-given wisdom from above. A doublet was found in Qumran: the large psalm scroll from Cave 11 includes the beginning of this Hebrew song, an alphabetic psalm where the units open with the letters of the alphabet in sequence. (Since the lower part of the scroll had decayed, the full psalm was not preserved.)

The Hebrew version is more bodily and sensual than the transmitted Greek text of Sirach. The text contains several double entendres, "foot" and "hand" serving as euphemisms for the male organ in both biblical and Qumran texts. Words and images having to do with desire and lovemaking symbolize the pious one's search both for wisdom and for blessings from God throughout his life.

On sensuality from Ben Sira to the Song of Songs, see pp. 199–200.

Revelation and Illumination to the Humble

You opened in me a fountain of knowledge

1QH[a] 10:5–21 (with parallels in 4QH[f])

[I thank you, L]ord,
that you have made straight in my heart all the deeds of iniquity,
and you have purified me [from all iniquities.]

You placed faithful guardians in the face of my distress,
righteous reprovers for all the violence [done to me. . . .]
[to bring healing] to the wound from the blow inflicted on me;
strong comforters [in my sorrow . . . ,]
announcing joy in place of my mourning and distress,
bringing a message of peace rather than reports of disasters—
strong [comforters] for my melting heart,
strengthening my spirit in the face of affliction.

To my uncircumcised lips you gave the proper reply;
you upheld my soul, strengthened my loins, and restored my power;
you maintained my steps in the realm of wickedness.

I have been a snare to those who rebel
but healing to those who repent of transgression,
discernment for the simple,
and steadfastness to the fearful of heart.
To traitors you have made of me a mockery and an object of scorn,
but a foundation of truth and understanding to the upright of way.

Because of the iniquity of the wicked,
I have become a slander on the lips of the ruthless;
the scoffers have gnashed their teeth.
I have become a mocking song for transgressors;
the assembly of the wicked has raged against me:
they have roared like turbulent seas,
and their towering waves were heaving up mud and slime.

But to the righteous elect
you have made me a banner,
a discerning interpreter of wonderful mysteries,
in order to test those who practice truth
and try those who love discipline.

To the interpreters of error I have been an opponent,
but a contender for all who see what is right.
I have become a zealous spirit
to all those who seek smooth things.
Like the sound of the roaring of many waters
all the deceivers thunder against me;
all their thoughts are devilish schemes.
They have cast towards the Pit
the life of the man in whose mouth you established knowledge,
in whose heart you placed understanding,
that he might open a fountain of knowledge
to all men of understanding.

The traitors exchanged true understanding
for the uncircumcised lips and alien tongue
of a people without understanding,
so that they will be ruined by their error.

In the middle of the Thanksgiving Hymns (columns 10–17) we find a row of psalms where the speaker is a self-confident teacher. He has been through trials and has been redeemed by God, who has called him to be an overflowing source of revelation to the simple ones. Calling these psalms "Teacher Hymns," some early scholars identified in them the voice of the "Teacher of Righteousness" (or "Legitimate Teacher"), the asserted priestly founder of the Qumran community.

Still denoting these songs as "Teacher Hymns," most scholars today see these texts as written "in the name of the Teacher" by later members of the community, possibly drawing on a tradition going back to the Teacher. This psalm and the next one belong to the Teacher Hymns. As the Thanksgiving Hymns were a widely used prayer book of the community, the partakers of the common prayer would have identified with the "I" of these psalms, and this would be particularly true for the priestly leader of the Community, "the Master."

The teacher of these songs has experienced tough persecution from his enemies. According to the Qumran commentary on Habakkuk (col. 11), the Wicked Priest (an antonym for a Hasmonean priestly ruler) came violently upon the Teacher of Righteousness on the latter's day of fasting (the Day of Atonement, which was dated differently in the respective calendars of these two priests).

This charismatic community leader has a remarkable self-confidence: he is "the man in whose mouth you established knowledge"; he has "opened a fountain of knowledge to all men of understanding." The self-understanding of the singer of the Teacher hymns can be compared with that of Jesus in the Gospels.

The designation used for opponents in the seventh stanza, "those who seek smooth things," is a derogatory term the Qumranites used for the early Pharisees. The term "smooth things" (*ḥalakot*) is a wordplay on *halakot* (legal rulings based on exegesis of biblical texts), a central feature in Pharisaic teaching. The conservative and priest-led Union disagreed with the more lay-oriented Pharisees on many issues.

This psalm and the one that follows contrast God's righteousness with sinful man, a creature of naught and vanity—an anthropology that can be compared with that of Paul. The God of mercy will nevertheless raise the humble ones from dust and make them stand before him. He makes them his true children and reveals to them his secrets.

You taught me wisdom by your truth

1QH[a] 15:29–36

I give thanks [to you, O Lord].
You taught me wisdom by your truth.
You made me know your wondrous mysteries,
your loving-kindness to a man [of vanity],
your great mercy to a failing heart.

Who is like you among the heavenly beings,
and who can match your truth?
Who, when judged, will stand righteous before you?
No spirit can reply to your rebuke;
none of the hosts can withstand your wrath.

Yet you make all your true sons stand forgiven before you;
you cleanse them of their faults through your great goodness,
by your abundant compassion you make them stand
in your presence forever and ever.

For you are an eternal God:
all your ways stand firm from eternal times;
there is none other beside you.
And what is a man of naught and vanity
that he should understand your wondrous mighty deeds?

THIS TEACHER HYMN CONTRASTS the righteousness of God with frail and sinful man. However, in his loving-kindness God cleanses earthly men, makes them his true sons who can stand in his presence, and reveals his mysteries to them.

You opened my ear to wondrous mysteries

1QH[a] 9:23–39

These things I know because of understanding that comes from you,
for you opened my ear to wondrous mysteries.
Yet I am a shape of clay kneaded in water,
a foundation of shame and a source of impurity,
a furnace of iniquity and an edifice of sin,
a straying and perverted spirit of no understanding,
and terrified by righteous judgments.

What can I say that is not foreknown,
and what can I utter that is not foretold?
All things are engraved before you
as an inscribed reminder for everlasting ages,
with the numbered cycles of all the years
and their appointed festivals;
they are not hidden or missing from your presence.

What shall a man say concerning his sin?
And how should he plead concerning his iniquities?
And how should he, a man of evil,
reply to righteous judgment?
For to you, God of knowledge,
belong all righteous deeds and true counsel,

but to the sons of men belong
the work of iniquity and deeds of deceit.

It is you who created breath for the tongue,
and you know its words;
you established the fruit of the lips
before they were spoken.
You set the words according to your measuring line,
and the flow of breath from the lips to meter.
You bring forth sounds according to your mysteries,
and the flow of breath according to their calculus,
that they may tell of your glory and recount your wonders
in all your faithful deeds and righteous judgments,
that your name be praised by the mouth of all who know you,
so that they, according to their understanding,
may bless you forever and ever.

In your compassion and mercy
you have strengthened the spirit of man in the face of affliction,
and the soul of [the poor] you have cleansed from great iniquity,
so that he may proclaim your wonders before all your creatures.

In their midst I will recite continually
the judgments by which I was scourged;
and to the sons of humankind, all your wonders,
by which you have shown yourself mighty
through me before the sons of men.

Hear, you wise men, you who ponder knowledge.
May those who are eager become firm in purpose,
and all who are straight increase prudence.

You righteous ones, put away iniquity.
All you perfect in the way, hold fast [to the covenant].
You who are afflicted with misery,
be patient and despise no righteous judgment.

In this community psalm, Essene and Qumranite anthropology is clearly articulated. From his inception man turns away from his Creator and cannot stand in God's presence. However, God can cleanse and forgive the members of his community on earth. He has created them to praise his name (the same idea is found in Eph 1:3–14). This psalm concludes with an exhortation to the pious to continue walking in the ways of God. We also sense the Essene view of God's sovereignty and foreknowledge: the ways of a man are preordained by God from eternal times.

You make me jealous for your ways

1QH[a] 6:19–33

Blessed are you, O Lord,
who has given understanding to the heart of your servant,
that he may have insight into all these things [. . .]
so that he can persevere against evil deeds
and bless with righteousness all who choose your goodwill;
that he [may love all] that you love
and abhor all that you hate.

You have given your servant insight
[into the ways of man and the] lot of humankind.
For according to their spirits you cast the lot for them
between good and evil;
you determined [their ways and their] recompence.

As for me, I know from the understanding that comes from you
that in your goodwill you increased a man's portion of your holy spirit.
Thus you draw him closer to the understanding of you.
And the closer he approaches, the more he is filled with zeal
against all evildoers and men of deceit.
For all who are near to you do not rebel against your command;
all who know you do not alter your words,
for you are righteous, and all your chosen ones are trustworthy.

All injustice and wickedness you will blot out forever,
and your righteousness will be revealed
before the eyes of all your creatures.

As for me, I know through your great mercy
and by the oath I pledged in my heart
that I should never sin against you
or do anything that is evil in your eyes.
And thus I bring into the Union all the men of my counsel.
I will cause each man to draw near
in accordance with his understanding
and according to the amount of his inheritance,
so will I love him.
I will not honor evil or acknowledge a bribe.
I will not barter your truth for riches,
nor any of your precepts for bribes.
According to the [ways] of a man
I will give him my love,
and as you remove him far from you,
so will I abhor him.
And I will not bring into your true council
any who turn away from your covenant.

This psalm is complete. It shows the sharp borderline between the Essene movement, which is under God's goodwill, and other Israelites, who walk in the way of perdition. In his dealings with others, the pious needs to reflect upon how God looks upon each and everyone, with grace and goodwill or with judgment and abhorrence.

This psalmist sees the ways of a man as preordained by God, who has determined their lots and placements on the scale between good and evil (second stanza). However, God can draw a man closer to him and thus increase his allotted portion of God's holy spirit (third stanza).

My eyes have gazed at eternal mysteries
Community Rule, 1QS 11:2–20

As for me, my justification is with God.
In his hand are the perfection of my way
and the uprightness of my heart.
He wipes out my transgression
through his righteousness.

For my light has sprung
from the source of his knowledge.
My eyes have gazed at his marvelous deeds,
and at the light of my heart, the mystery to come.
He, the everlasting, is the support of my right hand;
the way of my steps is the truth of God—
his might is the support of my right hand.
From the fountain of his righteousness is my justification,
from his wondrous mysteries is the light of my heart.

My eyes have at eternal mysteries:
wisdom concealed from men,
knowledge and understanding
hidden from the sons of men.
My heart has found a fountain of righteousness,
a storehouse of power, a spring of glory
hidden from the assembly of flesh.

This he has given to his chosen ones as an everlasting possession.
He has caused them to inherit the lot of the holy angels;
he has joined their assembly to the sons of heaven,
to be a Council of the Community,
a foundation of the building of holiness,
an everlasting seed-bearing plant throughout all ages to come.

As for me, I belong to wicked mankind,
to the company of unjust flesh.
My transgressions and iniquities,
my sins and my corrupt heart
belong to the company of worms
and to those who walk in darkness.

For a man's way is not his own;
man cannot establish his steps,
since justification is with God
and perfection of the way, in his hand.
All things come to pass by his knowledge;
he establishes all things by his design—
without him nothing is done.

And if I stumble,
the mercies of God are my eternal salvation.
If I stagger because of the sins of my flesh,
the righteousness of God is my justification forever.
He will deliver my soul from the pit
and direct my steps to the way.
He will draw me close by his grace,
will bring my justification by his mercy.
He will judge me in the righteousness of his truth,
in his great goodness atone for all my sins.

Through his righteousness he will cleanse me
of the uncleanness of man
and of the sins of the children of men,
that I may confess to God his righteousness,
and his majesty to the Most High.

Blessed are you, my God,
who opens the heart of your servant to knowledge.
Establish all his deeds in righteousness,
as it pleases you to do for the elect of mankind.
Grant that the son of your handmaid
may stand in your presence forever.
For without you no way is perfect,
without your will nothing is done.
There is none beside you to dispute your counsel,
to understand your holy design
and contemplate the depth of your mysteries
and the power of your might.

THE PSALM OPENS AS a hymn, with a reminder to always praise God. It continues by contrasting God's might with human weakness and reflects in awe on the inscrutable God who nevertheless reveals himself to the members of the Community down on earth.

As many of the Thanksgiving Hymns do, this psalm from the end of the Community Rule expresses the anthropology of the Qumran movement. For the Essenes, man's nature is perverted. The singer "belong[s] to wicked mankind" and "the company of unjust flesh." He has a corrupted heart and is bound to sin and iniquities: he belongs "to the company of worms / and to those who walk in darkness."

Sirach, Psalms of Solomon 6; 9; 16 (see pp. 35–36, 61–62, 65), and the Pharisees hold to a more optimistic anthropology. The Essenes read Ps 51:5 literally, and about all men, "Indeed, I was born guilty, a sinner when my mother conceived me." At the same time, the merciful God raises the sinner from dust and places him in the community of the children of light. As a member of the community, he has privileged access to the mysteries of God.

For a comparison with New Testament anthropology, see p. 201.

I am a source watering the garden

Sirach 24:30–34

As for me, I was like a canal from a river,
like a water channel running through a garden.
I said, "I will water my orchard and drench my flowerbeds."
And see, my canal has grown into a river,
and my river has grown into a sea.

I will make instruction shine forth like the dawn;
I shall send its light far and wide.
I shall pour out teaching like prophecy,
as a legacy to all future generations.
See that I have not toiled for myself alone,
but for all who are seeking wisdom.

THE MAIN PART OF Sir 24 is a beautiful poem put in the mouth of Lady Wisdom, who came forth from the mouth of the Creator and found her place of rest in the tabernacle and temple (24:1–22). Then follows a possibly later section equating eternal Wisdom with the Torah, the books of Moses (vv. 23–29). In the last verses, Ben Sira prides himself on being a God-given source of wisdom to men. Here we encounter a kind of prophetic self-consciousness. He knows that his teaching will illuminate his students and also be a light to future generations—and his book has indeed been treasured for centuries, by early rabbis, Karaite Jews, and countless Christians.

The Lord's Anointed

In the Hebrew Bible we find different images for the servants God will use as his elect tools on earth in the last days, in the time of redemption—redemption for Israel, for the nations, for the world. Texts in the Psalms and Prophets expect a king, a son of David, who will restore the glory of the nation of Israel. In some texts, he is portrayed as a warrior-king who will defeat neighboring nations. In others, he is peaceful and does not use tools of war; rather, God himself destroys arms and implements of war on earth. In some settings the king is described as a son of mankind, without heavenly qualities. However, in other of the texts the laws of nature are transcended in the messianic times, and an interpreter could ask if such promises are to be read symbolically or literally.

Then there are texts in Zechariah describing a princely ruler and an anointed priest side-by-side, as elect tools of redemption (4:1–14; 6:9–13). A couple of texts in Jeremia and Zechariah portray the end-time priest as the sole elect who will bring Israel to a renewed covenantal relation to God (Jer 30:18–24; Zech 13:7–9). In the Isaianic Book of Consolation (chapters 40–66), a servant of God will bring freedom to the nations. This servant might be described as a worldly ruler, as a prophet, or as a suffering servant who will bring atonement to his people.

In the composite chapter 7 of Daniel, the vision shows a son of humankind coming with the clouds of heaven, being brought before God the ancient of days, given rulership on earth as in heaven, and all nations will serve or worship him (the Aramaic verb *palaḥ* can carry both meanings). Some scholars see in this enigmatic figure the royal messiah, others disagree. In the last section of Dan 7, however, there is no son of man, while God's elect tool on earth in the struggle against evil is his people, assisted by the angels—a collective messianism.

From the third century onwards, the small temple province Judea repeatedly experienced wars and tribulations. From 170 BCE, the king ruling from Antioch, Antiochus Epiphanes, used violent means to make the Judeans true members of the Hellenistic culture. After ravaging Jerusalem, he desecrated the temple, outlawed traditional Judaism, proscribed circumcision and forced Jews to eat pork. This led to a Judean revolt. Under the leadership of the Maccabean brothers, Judean guerilla fighters caused the Syrian armies to retreat. After three years fighting, they liberated most of Jerusalem so that they could cleanse and rededicate the temple in 164 BCE—the beginning of the Hanukka festival. The leader of the revolt, Judah the Maccabee, was killed in 160. His brothers Jonathan and Simon forcefully extended the borders of Judea, and Simon's son John Hyrcanus (134–105) led Judea to full independence. The Maccabean brothers were of a priestly family and took over the high-priestly office alongside being rulers of the nation, with time also claiming the title king of Judea. From Simon onwards the family is called Hasmonean, possibly after the name of an ancestor, and Simon initiates a hereditary dynasty.

These times of unrest, suffering and war saw a flowering of different hopes of salvation. Some hailed the Hasmoneans as messianic forerunners of final redemption. Others criticized them for taking on the double office of ruler and high priest, suppression of oppositional groups, or cruel rulership.

Among the dissident voices were the Essenes—in the Dead Sea Scrolls we find a variety of hopes for figures of redemption: a suffering servant in the role of a priest with a unique teaching voice, a king and a priest alongside each other, a son of David in conjunction with the Qumranite community, a messiah with heavenly authority over mankind, an angelic redeemer who from heaven would fight the evil forces and redeem the sons of light on earth, or the elect nation as God's earthly tool in the way toward salvation.

He set me as prince of his people

Ps 151A, 11QPs[a] 151:3–12

Hallelujah! Of David, son of Jesse.
I was smaller than my brothers, youngest of my father's sons.
He made me shepherd of his sheep and ruler over his goats.

My hands fashioned a pipe, my fingers a lyre,
and I glorified the Lord.
I said to myself, the mountains do not testify to him,
the hills do not talk about him.
Trees, echo my words! Sheep, echo my deeds!
Who can proclaim and who can declare the deeds of the Lord?
God has seen all, he has heard all, and he listens to all.

He sent his prophet to anoint me, Samuel, to magnify me.
My brothers went out to meet him:
beautiful of figure, beautiful of appearance.
They were tall of stature with beautiful hair,
yet the Lord God did not choose them.

No, he sent for me
and took me who followed the flock
and anointed me with holy oil.
He set me as prince of his people
and ruler over the children of his covenant.

THIS POEM, PUT INTO the mouth of King David, testifies to the hope for a new anointed king of the seed of David, a hope still alive in third- and second-century Judea. The second stanza portrays David as a musician who plays and sings to the glory of God. These lines allude to David as originator of the Psalter and spiritual father of the temple singers. In the last stanzas David sings about how he was elected and anointed to be the prince of God's chosen people.

The text follows the more elaborate Hebrew version from Qumran, not the shorter Greek text preserved in the Septuagint.

On Ps 151, see pp. 201–2.

Judah the Maccabee, the Lion of Judah

1 Maccabees 3:3–9

Judah extended the fame of his people.
He put on the breastplate like a giant,
girded on his war harness and waged battles,
protecting the camp by his sword.
He was like a lion in his deeds,
like a lion's cub roaring for prey.

He searched out and pursued those who broke the law,
he burned those who troubled his people.
Lawbreakers shrank back for fear of him,
all the evildoers were confounded,
and deliverance prospered by his hand.

He brought bitterness to many kings
and rejoicing to Jacob by his deeds,
his memory is blessed forever.

He went through the cities of Judah,
he destroyed the ungodly out of the land,
turning away wrath from Israel.
His name resounded to the ends of the earth,
he gathered in those who were lost.

Judah the Maccabee was the leader of the Maccabean revolt against Syrian oppression of the Judeans and their faithfulness to Israelite tradition, a revolt that led to the creation of an independent Judean state ruled by the Hasmonean family.

This laudatory poem describes Judah in messianic colors. Judah "was like a lion in his deeds, like a lion's cub roaring for prey"—an echo of the blessing of Judah in Gen 49:9. Judah the Maccabee is thus the "Lion of Judah" of his time. The transition from a ruler of the "tribe of Judah" in Gen 49:8–12 to the "warrior Judah the Maccabee" is easily done; his acts align with the fighter envisioned in Gen 49:8–9. The proclamations that "his memory is blessed forever" and "his name resounded to the ends of the earth" recall the messianic psalm 72 (cf. Ps 72:8, 17). "He gathered in those who were lost" would recall prophecies of the ingathering of the dispersed ones (Ezek 34:12–13; 36:24; Mic 4:6). The description of Judah's armor recalls that of Goliath, Saul, and David (1 Sam 17:5–7, 38–39).

On 1 Maccabees, see pp. 202–4.

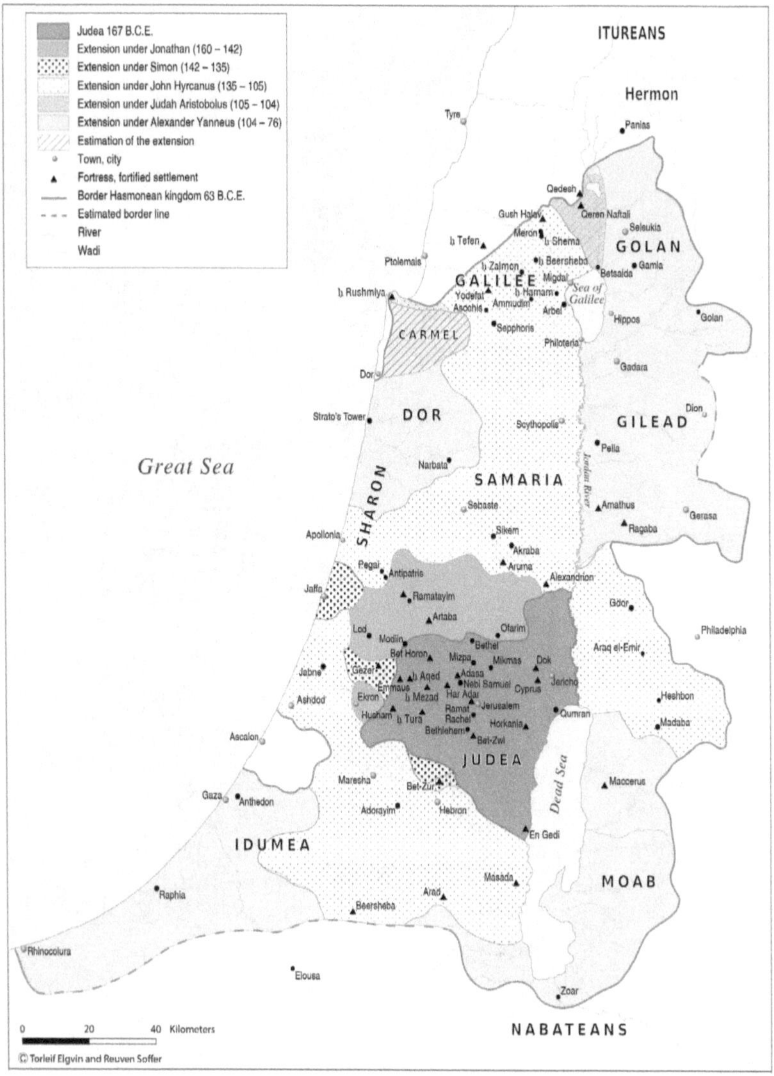

Fig. 4: Map of the expansion of the Hasmonean state. Copyright © 2022 Reuven Soffer and Torleif Elgvin.

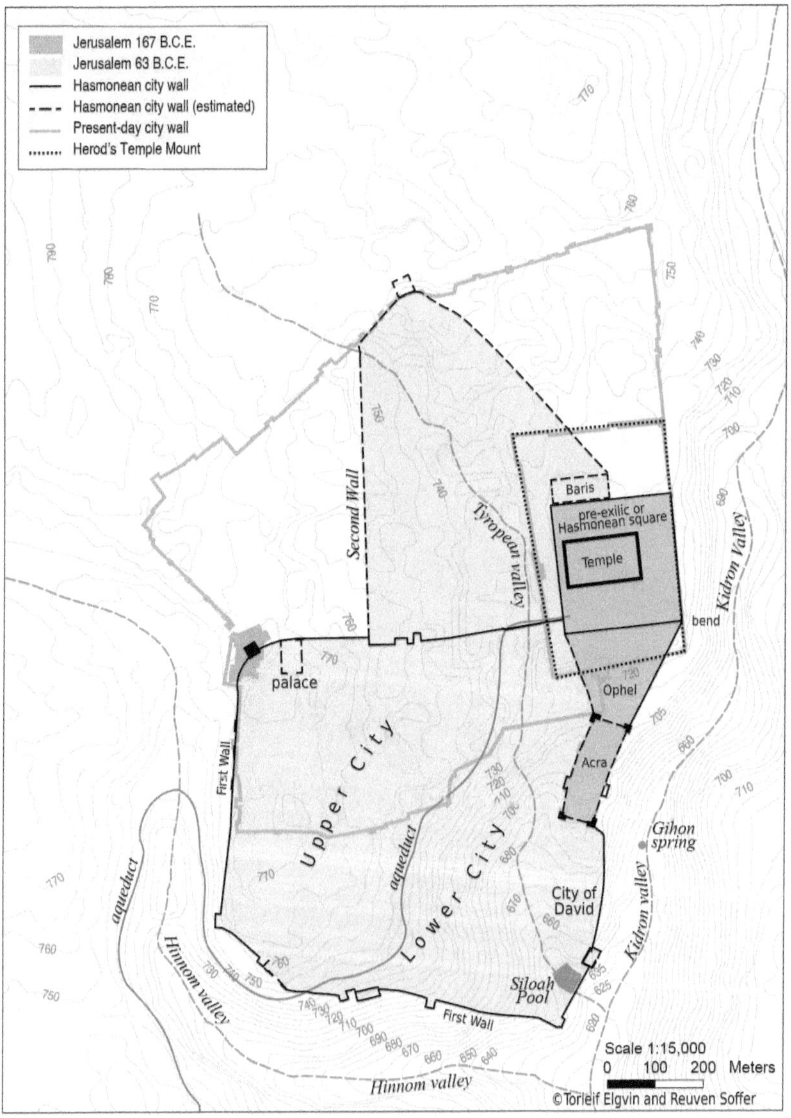

Fig. 5: The growth of Hasmonean Jerusalem.
Copyright © 2022, Reuven Soffer and Torleif Elgvin.

Prince Simon made peace in the land

1 Maccabees 14:4–15

The land was at peace throughout the days of Simon.
He sought the good of his nation,
his rule was pleasing to them,
as was his fame throughout his life.

With great honor he took Joppe and made it his harbor,
an entranceway to the islands of the sea.
He extended the borders of his nation
and gained full control in the land.
He gathered a host of captives,
he conquered Gezer, Beth-zur, and the Citadel,
and cast out the unclean things from it,
no one could resist him.

They farmed their land in peace,
the land gave its produce,
the trees of the plain their fruit.
Old men sat at ease in the streets,
they talked together of good things,
the young men put on splendid military attire.
He supplied the towns with food,
furnished them with means of defense,

his fame resounded to the ends of the earth.
He established peace in the land,
and Israel knew great joy.

Each man sat under his own vine and fig tree,
there was none to make them afraid.
No enemy was left in the land to fight them,
the kings were crushed in those days.
He gave help to all the needy among his people,
he strove to observe the law
and cleared away every lawless and wicked man.
He gave new splendor to the temple,
replenishing it with sacred vessels.

SIMON WAS THE LAST of the first generation of the Maccabean family to rule the country (142–134 BCE). He initiated large building projects in Jerusalem, including extension and renovation of the temple area, and drove the Seleucid garrison out of the provocative Citadel, located close to the temple.

Simon claimed full authority in the land. 1 Macc 14:41–47 renders a decree adopted by a common assembly, where Simon (and subsequently his descendants) is declared ruler and high priest for all times. Priests and laymen are forbidden to initiate gatherings without his permission—reflecting that oppositional groups such as the Essenes were suppressed.

The ancient sources suggested that all the nation supported the Hasmoneans' military expansion of the bourgeoning Judean state. But oppositional voices such as the Essenes could argue against Simon's authoritarian rule, and early Pharisaic circles were critical to the Hasmoneans claiming both the throne and the high priesthood.

The laudatory poem describes Simon's rule as a time of peace: he saved the nation from its enemies, gave Judea safe borders, and provided access to the Mediterranean when he conquered Joppe (=Jaffa) with its harbor. The poem alludes to scriptural promises such as Ps 2:9; 72:8; 89:25; 110:2, 5; Isa 11:4; Mic 4:4; 5:4–5; Zech 9:10.

On Simon's reign and this laudation of Simon, see pp. 204–5.

Blessing upon a Hasmonean King

4QApocryphal Psalm and Prayer, 448 2–3

Awake, Holy One, for King Jonathan
and all the congregation of your people Israel,
who is dispersed to the four winds of heaven!
Let peace be on all of them and on your kingdom!
May your name be blessed!

In your love I am firmly founded [and will sing]
all through the day until evening.
From he[aven look down,]
come close and be in [their midst]!
Remember [your people] with blessing and m[ercy]!
[Have compassion], for your name that is called [over them]
[and over] the kingdom, to bless [them].
[Visit them] on the day of war
and b[ring victory] to Jonathan the kin[g and your people Israel!]
May [your name] be ble[s]sed!

Scholars were astonished when this text—a blessing upon a Hasmonean king—was deciphered in 1992, knowing that the Qumran community identified themselves in sharp opposition to the Jerusalem leadership. Jonathan was the Hebrew name of Alexander Jannaeus, ruler, king and high priest 104–76 BCE. Jannaeus took the title king and conquered large territories, his Judea is the largest Israelite state in history. However, his reign was also marked by sharp divisions within the nation, in the 90s he was in armed conflict with Pharisaic circles, who wanted him to give up the high-priestly office. A Qumran biblical commentary calls him "the Lion of Wrath." The first column of this scroll—of which only the beginning was preserved—was a psalm that praised God's dwelling in the temple. Could a deposed Pharisee have brought such a scroll from Jerusalem to Qumran?

The blessing upon king Jonathan and his people shows how the Judeans longed for the soon-to-come fulfilment of biblical promises. For this singer, the presence of God can be sensed in Jonathan's wars and victories. In the second verse, he uses the same term on Jonathan's kingship as he uses on God's kingdom in the first.

On this scroll, see pp. 205–6.

Fig. 6: 4Q448. The scroll with the blessing upon King Jonathan. Note the thong used for binding. Courtesy of the Leon Levy Dead Sea Scrolls Digital Library, Israel Antiquities Authority. Photo: Shai Halevi (B-295803).

Fig. 7: A coin of Alexander Jannaeus from around 85 BCE. The obverse has an anchor encircled by the Greek for "King Alexander" (*Alexandrou basileos*). The reverse has a diadem around the sun or the star of Jacob (Num 24:17) with the Hebrew for "King Jonathan." Courtesy of CNG Coins.

Raise up their king, the son of David

Psalms of Solomon 17:4–9, 20–46

4It was you, Lord, who chose David to be king over Israel,
you swore to him about his descendants forever,
that you would not cut off his royal house.
But because of our iniquities sinners rose against us,
they attacked us and drove us out.

Those to whom you did not make the promise,
they came as violent robbers,
They did not honor your glorious name.
With pride they set up their own royal house,
they despoiled the throne of David with arrogant shouting.
But you, O God, will overthrow them,
and uproot their descendants from the land.
A man from the nations will rise against them,
you will repay them according to their sins,
it will happen to them according to their deeds.
9God will show them no mercy,
and hunt down their descendants so that no one will escape.

20From their leader to the common people
they committed every kind of sin,
the king broke the law, the judges were disobedient,
and the people was sinning.

[21]Look Lord, and raise up for them their king,
the son of David, to rule over your servant Israel
in the time that you know, O God.
Gird him with strength to destroy unrighteous rulers,
to purge Jerusalem from gentiles who trample her down to destruction.
Gird him with wisdom and righteousness,
to drive out sinners from the inheritance,
to smash the arrogance of sinners like a potter's jar,
to shatter their foundation with an iron rod,
to destroy lawless nations with the word of his mouth.
At his warning, nations will flee from his presence,
he will condemn sinners for the thoughts of their hearts.

He will gather a holy people and lead it in righteousness.
He will judge the tribes of the people
who have been made holy by the Lord his God.
He will not tolerate unrighteousness among them
or any wicked man to live with them.
For he shall know them, that they are all children of their God.
He will distribute them throughout the land according to their tribes,
no alien or foreigner will live near them.

He will judge peoples and nations in wisdom and justice,
gentile nations will serve under his yoke.
He will glorify the Lord all through the land,
and purify Jerusalem to be holy as it was in the beginning.
Nations will come from the ends of the earth to see his glory,
to bring as gifts her children who had been exiled,
to see the glory of the Lord who has glorified her.

He will be a righteous king over them, taught by God.
There will be no wickedness among them in his days,
everyone will be holy, their king will be the Lord's messiah.
He will not rely on cavalry with sword and bow,
nor will he collect gold and silver for war,
nor will he build up hope among men for a day of battle.
The Lord himself is his king, he has a strong hope in his God.
He shall be compassionate to all the nations
who stand reverently before him.

He will strike the land with the word of his mouth forever,
he will bless the Lord's people with wisdom and happiness.
He will be free from sin so that he can rule a great people.
He will expose leaders and drive out sinners by the strength of his word.
He will not weaken in his days, relying upon his God,
for God will make him powerful by holy spirit,
wise in intelligent counsel, with strength and righteousness.
The blessing of the Lord will be his strength,
he will not weaken, and his hope will be in the Lord.

Who can stand up against him,
mighty in actions and strong in the fear of God?
He will be a faithful and righteous shepherd of the Lord's flock,
he will not let any of them weaken in their pasture.
He will lead them justly,
there will be no arrogance among them,
so that no one will oppress his neighbor.

This is the beauty of the king of Israel,
acknowledged by God to be raised over the house of Israel

to lead and discipline it.
His words will be purer than refined gold,
he will implement justice when the clans assemble,
the tribes that are sanctified.
His words will be as the words of the holy angels
among men who are sanctified.

Blessed are those born in those days,
to see the good fortune of Israel
that God will bring when he assembles the tribes.
May God hasten his mercy to Israel,
may he shield us from the contamination of defiled enemies.
The Lord himself is our king forevermore!

THIS IS ONE OF the youngest texts in this section on the anointed, written in the mid-first century BCE. Verses 4–9 lament the decay under the last Hasmonean rulers and continues with God's judgment on the Hasmoneans by the hand of Pompey ("a man from the nations").

From v. 21 appears a beautiful hymn on the coming messianic king, which abounds with echoes of Davidic and messianic biblical texts, not the least Ps 72. Different from the Hasmonean warlords, this king will not rely on a strong army. Nevertheless, God will make gentile nations subordinate to him. They will stand before him as vassal kings before an emperor, and delight in his compassion. He will be a true shepherd for his people—as it was described in Davidic promises.

For more on this messianic psalm, see pp. 206–7.

Heaven and earth will obey his messiah

4QMessianic apocalypse, 4Q521 frg. 2 col. 2:1–13.

1 [For hea]ven and earth will obey his anointed,
[and nothing th]at is in them will turn away
from the rules of the holy angels.

3 Be strong, you who seek the Lord, when you serve him!
Indeed, in this you will find the Lord, all you who hope in your heart
that the Lord will see to the pious and call the righteous by name.

6 Over the poor his spirit will hover,
with his strength he will restore the faithful.
From his eternal royal throne he will honor the pious,
he who sets prisoners free, opens the eyes of the blind,
and raises up those who are bo[wed down].

Forever I shall cling to those who set their hope to the Lord,
by his loving kindness h[e will come near(?)],
the fru[it of good dee]ds to a neighbor shall not tarry.

The Lord shall do glorious things that have never been done, just as he said.
For he shall heal the badly wounded, revive the dead,
and proclaim good news to the afflicted.

He shall satis[fy the poo]r,
guide the uprooted, and enrich the hungry, [. . .]

This vision of the messianic age draws on biblical texts such as Dan 7, Ps 146, and 1 Sam 2. In the first two lines we encounter a messiah with heavenly powers, assisted by his serving angels, while lines 3–5 speak to the pious community on earth. From line 6 follows a description of the signs of the messianic age. God is the acting subject, but his intervention for the lowly ones on earth follows the heavenly enthronement of the princely messiah (cf. line 1).

As many interpreters observe, this text (or the tradition it represents) receives sequels in the gospels, Matt 11:2–6 // Luke 7:18–23; 4:18–19. However, few have noted that the closest textual echo of the words "[For hea]ven and earth will obey his anointed . . . when you serve him" is the last words of Jesus in Matt 28:18: "All authority in heaven and on earth has been given to me," preceded by "they worshiped him" (28:17).

On 4QMessianic apocalypse, see pp. 207–8.

Fig. 8: Messianic Apocalypse, 4Q521 frg. 2. The text appears in the middle column, from the top onwards. Courtesy of the Leon Levy Dead Sea Scrolls Digital Library, Israel Antiquities Authority. Photo: Shai Halevi (B-513138).

The end-time priest and the end-time prince

Messianic Rule, 1QSa 2:11–22.

This is the order of the assembly of the men of renown,
[summoned] for the gathering, for the council of the community:
when God fathers the messiah among them:
[the Priest,] head of the entire congregation of Israel, shall enter first,
trailed by all his brothers,[the sons of] Aaron,
the priests [summoned] for the gathering of the men of renown.
They are to sit before him by rank.

Then the messiah of Israel may enter,
and the heads of their thousands are to sit before him by rank,
according to their standing in their camps and their marches.
Last, all the heads of the congregation's c[lans,]
with their sages [and wise men] shall sit before them by rank.

When they gather[at the tabl]e of the community,
[to set out bread and new]wine and arrange the table of the community,
[and to pour the] new wine for drinking,
nobody [should stretch out] his hand
to the first portion of the bread or [new wine] before the Priest.
For he shall bless the first portion of the bread and the new wine
and be the first to [stretch out] his hand for the bread.

And afterwards, the messiah of Israel
shall stretch out his hands to the bread.
Finally, the entire congregation of the community shall bless,
each one according to his rank.
This regulation shall govern every meal,
provided at least ten men are assembled together.

NOT A STRICTLY POETIC text, this vision of the future is included because of its expressed teaching on two messiahs. The expected ruler is called "messiah of Israel," while the end-time high priest only appears as "the Priest."

When Israel's messiah appears, he will first reveal himself to God's elect community, i.e., the Qumran movement, and be celebrated in a festival meal where all are sitting according to their rank. In the liturgical order, the Priest comes before the royal messiah. While this festive table liturgy seems rather peaceful, column 1 of 1QSa portrays the royal messiah as fighting Israel's enemies.

The expression "when God fathers the messiah" (lit., "when God causes the messiah to be born") refers to Ps 2:7: in the act of coronation God "conceives" the new king and adopts him as son.

On the Messianic Rule, see pp. 208–9.

You judge the nations by the power of your mouth

Rule of Blessings, 1QSb 5:20–28

The Master shall bless the Prince of the Congregation, [. . .]
he shall renew for him the covenant of the Union,
that he may establish the kingdom of God's people forever,
that "with righteousness he may judge the poor
and decide with equity for the lowly of the land," (Isa 11:4),
that he may walk perfectly before him in all the ways of truth,
and establish his holy covenant
at the time of affliction of those who seek God.

May the Lord raise you up to everlasting heights,
a mighty tower upon a raised rampart.
May you "strike the land with the rod of your mouth,
and kill the wicked with the breath of your lips." (Isa 11:4)
"May he give you a spirit of counsel and everlasting might,
a spirit of knowledge and fear of God." (Isa 11:2)
"May righteousness be the belt around your waist
and faithfulness the belt around your loins." (Isa 11:4–5)

"May he make your horns iron and your hoofs bronze." (Mic 4:13)
May you gore like a bull . . . and trample the nations
like mud in the streets, for God has established you
as a scepter to the rulers . . . and all nations shall serve you.
He shall strengthen you with his holy name,

you shall be as a lion among the beasts of the forest
that devours his prey with none to rescue.
Your swift steeds shall spread out upon the earth.

The Rule of Blessings is the second appendix to the Community Rule from Cave 1. Five fragmentary columns contain various liturgical blessings. This text represents the blessing of the princely messiah, the son of David, who will stand forth in the end-time. While the anointed priest has a role also in the heavens (see the next text), the job description of the princely messiah is earthly, in Israel and among the nations.

The messianic prophecy about the shoot of Jesse from Isa 11 is the main text of reference for the second stanza. The following horns of iron and hoofs of bronze are drawn from Mic 4:13, a promise spoken to the humiliated daughter Zion about her coming war against and victory over the nations. "All nations shall serve you" echoes the messianic Ps 72 (v. 11). Being "a scepter to the rulers" he will fulfil Balaam's messianic prophecy about the Star of Jacob (Num 24:17). The "lion among the beasts of the forest that devours his prey" echoes Jacob's oracle on the lion of Judah (Gen 49:9).

May you be like an angel serving in his holy habitation

Rule of Blessings, 1QSb 3:22–28; 4:22–28

The Master shall bless the priests, the sons of Zadok,
whom God has chosen to confirm his covenant forever,
to inquire into all his precepts in the midst of his people,
and to instruct them as he commanded.
They have truly held fast to his covenant,
righteously observing all his statutes
and walking according to the ways of his choice.

May the Lord bless you from his holy habitation.
May he set you as a glorious ornament in the midst of the holy angels.
May he renew the covenant of eternal priesthood for you.
May he grant you a place in his holy habitation.
May he judge all the nobles by your deeds,
and all the princes of the nations by the words flowing from your lips.
May he grant as your portion the first fruits of all delights,
may he bless by your hand the counsel of all flesh.

He has chosen you [. . .] to place you at the head of the holy angels,
and bless by your hand the men of God's community,
not by the hand of princes or by the hand of a man toward his fellow.
May you be like an angel of the presence in the holy habitation,
for the glory of the God of hosts [. . .]

May you attend upon the service in his royal temple,
and decree destiny with the angels of the presence,
to be in communion with the holy angels
for everlasting ages and time without end,
for all his judgments are truth.

May he make you holy among his people,
to illumine the world with knowledge forever,
and enlighten the face of many [with wisdom].
May he make you a diadem of the Holy of Holies,
for you are sanctified to him,
and you shall glorify his name and his holiness.

THE FIRST TWO STANZAS of this liturgical blessing are to be proclaimed over every legitimate priest, while the last ones are intended for the high priest. To the job description of the priests belongs teaching the people God's statutes. The words of blessing create a bridge between God's heavenly abode and the earthly priests of the temple—the physical temple or the spiritual "temple of men" of the Union. The priests enjoy a spiritual connection with the heavenly sanctuary, there is "a place for you in the holy habitation."

The high priest officiates simultaneously on earth and in heaven. Officiating on earth, he is at the same time spiritually present with the heavenly angels above, performing an incense offering in the heavenly sanctuary. He is even placed at the head of the holy angels. We may compare a later rabbinic tradition noting that God has to his disposal myriads of angels, but only one high priest on earth, whose ministry on Yom Kippur secures that atonement may be made for the people of Israel.

The high priest of the Rule of Blessings will enlighten God's people and illumine the world of nations—cf. the next text that prophecies that through the end-time priest the everlasting sun will shine all over the earth and engulf evil and darkness.

In the Rule of Blessings we cannot identify terminology characteristic of the writings originating in the Union. Therefore, these blessings may represent ideas shared by the priests and Levites of the temple.

He shall atone for the children of his generation

4QApocryphon of Levi, 4Q541 frg. 9, 1:1–7

[all] the children of his generation [. . .]
[and great is] his wisdom.
He shall make atonement for all the children of his generation,
he shall be sent to all the children of his people.
His words are like the words of heaven,
his teaching like the will of God.
His everlasting sun will shine,
its fire will give warmth unto the ends of the earth.
It will shine on darkness,
darkness will vanish from the earth and mist from the dry land.

They will speak malicious words against him, and many lies,
invent fables about him and speak all kinds of shameful things
about him.
His generation will be evil and perverted
so that it will be [rejected.]
His time of office will be marked by lies and violence,
in his days the people will go astray and be confounded.

THIS FRAGMENT COMES FROM an Aramaic writing about the biblical patriarch Levi, the ancestor of the priests. Some of the fragments talk about a priest that God will send in the last days.

This text sees the end-time high priest as a tool for universal renewal: the first stanza describes the priest and his unique ministry toward his people. He teaches with authority—teaching belonged to the job description of the priests. He will carry forth an atoning sacrifice not only for his nation, but for all mankind. Readers of the text would imagine a bloody animal sacrifice brought forth in the temple.

His ministry will lead to a cosmic renewal—all mankind and all the earth are in view. Until the ends of the earth, darkness will disappear, and his sun (God's or the priest's) will radiate throughout the world—this may be the sun that will shine 24/7 as a sign of the new creation (Zech 14:6–8).

The second paragraph looks back to an earlier phase in the priest's career. He is a victim of slander and persecution from adversaries in his own people. Allusions to Isa 53 show that the image of the Suffering Servant colors the description of this end-time messianic priest.

On this "Levi" scroll, see pp. 209–11.

God has enthroned me in the heavenly council

Self-Glorification Hymn, 4Q491c frg. 11:5–11

[To me is given] a mighty throne
in the angelic council forever.
No king of yore can sit on it,
neither can their nobles.
Who can be compared [to me]?
None can compare to my glory,
none has been exalted save myself,
and none can accompany me.

[ ] I am reckoned with the angels,
my dwelling is in the holy council.
My desire is not of the flesh,
for everything precious to me
is in the glory of the holy habitation.

Who has been despised like me,
yet who is like me in my glory?
[ ], who has borne afflictions like me,
who compares to me in enduring evil?

Never have I been instructed,
yet no teaching compares to mine.

Who could cut off my [words]?
And who could measure the flow of my speech?
Who can associate with me and compare with my judgment?

[ ] For I am reckoned with the angels
my glory is with the sons of the king.
Neither with gold nor refined gold
[I will be adorned . . .]

THIS TEXT, CALLED THE Self-Glorification Hymn, is preserved in two copies of the Thanksgiving Hymns and two texts from the War Scroll tradition. Here I follow the recension in one of the latter. Still alive on earth, the speaker of the hymn is elevated by God and receives a seat in the heavenly council. He has experienced opposition and suffering on earth, and his teaching is essential, for Israel and indirectly for all the world.

The imagined singer could be the priestly founder of the Qumran movement in the second century, the Teacher of Righteousness. Or more likely, this Teacher functioned as type for the end-time high priest.

On the Self-Glorification Hymn, see pp. 211–12.

His star shall rise in heaven

Testament of Levi 18

Vengeance from the Lord shall come upon my descendants
and the priesthood will come to an end.
But then the Lord will raise up for them a new priest
to whom all the words of the Lord will be revealed.
He shall judge the earth with truth for many days.
His star shall raise in heaven like a king's,
kindling the light of knowledge as the sun illuminates the day.
He shall be extolled by the whole world of men.
He will shine as the sun upon the earth
and take away darkness from under heaven,
there shall be peace over all the earth.

In his days the heavens shall rejoice greatly,
the earth shall be glad
and the clouds filled with joy.
The glorious angels of the Lord's presence
will rejoice over him,
and knowledge of the Lord will be poured out
on the earth as water covers the sea.

Heaven will be opened,
from the glorious temple above he will be sanctified

by a fatherly voice, as from Abraham to Isaac.
The glory of the Most High will be poured upon him,
the spirit av understanding and holiness shall rest upon him.

For he shall share the majesty of the Lord
with his true children forever,
he shall have no successor throughout generations.
During his priesthood the nations shall increase in knowledge,
they shall be illuminated by the grace of the Lord,
but Israel shall be diminished because of her ignorance
and darkened by her grief.

During his priesthood sin shall cease
the iniquity of ungodly men shall pause,
while the righteous shall find their rest in him.
He shall bind Beliar and open the gates of paradise
and remove the sword threatening them since Adam,
he will grant the saints to eat of the tree of life.

The spirit of holiness shall be upon them,
he shall grant his children authority to trample on evil spirits.
The Lord will rejoice in his children,
he will be pleased by his beloved ones forever.
Abraham, Isaac, and Jacob will rejoice,
I will jubilate, and all the saints will be clothed in righteousness.

The Testaments of the Twelve Patriarchs is a collection of exhortations and "prophecies" about the end-times, put in the mouth of the sons of Jacob as admonition to their sons before they passed away. There is a long literary history behind the book, stretching back to the second century BCE. By the mid-second century CE, a Jewish-Christian editor polished the book and added many small interpolations, thus "clarifying" many references to Jesus. Thus, the final text is a mixture of Jewish and Christian material.

While the Testament of Judah expects a royal messiah of David's seed, this text from the Testament of Levi foresees a messiah from the priestly tribe of Levi. The promise that "his star shall raise in heaven like a king's" refers to the prophecy of Balaam that "a star shall rise from Jacob, a scepter go up from Israel" (Num 24:17)—a prophecy that would be called forth in Matthew 2, by messianic pretenders during the great Jewish revolt, and by supporters of Bar Kosba (=Bar Kokhba, the "Son of the Star"), the leader of the second-century revolt against the Romans (132–136 CE).

When the Testament of Levi received its final form, one knew that Bar Kokhba's revolt had failed with catastrophic consequences for the nation of Israel. Nevertheless, the Jewish-Christian editor of the testaments looked forward to a millennium where the messiah would reign from Jerusalem. Yet later, a gentile and more anti-Jewish scribe would add a final clause, "Israel shall be diminished because of her ignorance and darkened by her grief."

On Testament of Levi, see pp. 212–13.

Melchizedek—the heavenly redeemer

11QMelchizedek (11Q13) 2:4–25

In the last days, [Melchize]dek,
[the head of God's heavenly armies],
will bring the captives back,
those who are are of his inheritance,
liberty shall be proclaimed to them,
he will free them from [the debt of] all their iniquities [. . .]
At the last D[ay of Atone]ment [. . .],
atonement will be made for all the sons of [light,]
the men of Mel[chi]zedek's lot [. . .]

For this is the time decreed for the year of favor of Melchizedek
and [his] arm[ies, the nati]on of the holy ones of God.
The psalms of David write about him,
The god-like one shall [sta]nd in the ass[embly of the heavenly,
and judge in the midst of the quasi-divine (Ps 82:1).
About him it is said, the god-like one shall judge the nations (Ps 7:9).
And he, Melchizedek, will carry out the vengeance of God's judgments.
[On that day he will free them from the hand of] Belial
and all the s[pirits of his lot.]
All the angels [of justice] shall come to his help,
he [will muster] them all [. . .]

This is the day of peace foresaid by Isaiah the prophet,
How beautiful on the mountains
are the feet of the messenger who announces peace,
the messenger of good who announces salvation
and says to Zion, your god-like one has been made king [. . .] (Isa 52:7)
About him it is written, your god-like one has been made king, [. . .]
And your god-like one is [the angelic Melchizedek],
[who will) free [them from the han]d of Belial.

This text does not appear in a strict poetic form. It is included here because it documents a particular kind of messianism, with Melchizedek, God's angelic viceroy, as the main actor. When time comes for the last jubilee year and its Day of Atonement, Melchizedek will provide atonement for the children of light, those who are of his lot. As in Luke 4:16–22, the year of favor promised in Isaiah 61:1–4 will unfold, the community on earth will be saved from the power of Belial and receive forgiveness and peace.

Melchizedek, a figure known from Gen 14 and Ps 110, is here understood as the head of God's heavenly armies, an angel performing priestly service before the heavenly throne. For this priestly author, Gen 14 likely described an earthly visit by this heavenly priest and prince. Some biblical references to *ʾel* and *ʾelohim* (a term that can mean God, angel, or heavenly being) are here read about Melchizedek (Ps 82:1; 7:9; Isa 52:7; 61:2). I have above used "the god-like one" for *ʾel* and *ʾelohim*.

As I see it, a similar understanding of Melchizedek as a priestly angel is presupposed in the letter to the Hebrews, not the least in chapter 7, where Melchizedek prefigures Jesus and his end-time sacrifice.

On 11QMelchizedek and Hebrews, see pp. 213–15.

The End of Days
and the World to Come

The prophets of the Hebrew Bible looked forward to a time of redemption for Israel, following times of judgment and tribulations. According to some of these texts, God will also renew the nations and all the earth.

With Judea and Jerusalem experiencing war and ravaging in the tumultuous years in the late third century, and again under the blasphemous king Antiochus in the 160s, the Judeans longed for a new future and time of redemption. Some of these texts have a dualistic world view: there are evil spiritual forces fighting against God and his people. The time of tribulation will end when God judges darkness and evil and renews the people of Israel. To fulfil his plan on earth, the Lord will use a particular part of the people, a righteous remnant who listens to his voice, obeys his will, and receives new revelation about the mysteries of God.

Some texts focus on the coming judgment in heaven and on earth, while others describe the overflowing fertility that will be in the land and the abundance of blessings given to the sons of men. In some of the poems and visions, only Israel is in focus, while other poets know that God's will is a renewal of all mankind.

God will descend and judge the world

1 Enoch 1:3–9

The Great Holy One will come forth from his dwelling,
the eternal God will tread from there upon Mount Sinai.
He will be revealed with his great army,
from heavens he will appear in the strength of his might.

All the Watchers will fear and quake,
those who are hiding at the ends of the earth will sing.
The ends of the earth will be shaken,
trembling and great fear will seize the Watchers unto the ends of the earth.

The high mountains will be shaken, fall and break apart,
the high hills will be made low and melt like wax before the fire.
The earth will be rent asunder,
everything on the earth will perish,
there will be judgment on all.

With the righteous he will make peace,
over the chosen there will be protection,
upon them will be mercy.
They will all be God's,
and he will grant them his good pleasure.

Light will shine upon them,
he will make peace with them.

Behold, he comes with the myriads of his holy angels
to execute judgment on all,
to destroy all the wicked and convict all flesh
for all the wicked deeds they have done,
for the haughty words that wicked sinners spoke against him.

THIS VISION OF THE end-time appearance of God opens the first and oldest section of 1 Enoch, the Book of Watchers (see pp. 175–77). Only twenty words of this poem are preserved in two small fragments of a Qumran scroll (4QEn[a]). Large parts of the Book of Watchers go back to the third century, while the introductory chapters derive from the tumultuous years before the Maccabean uprising.

1 Enoch 1–5 in general, and this poem in particular, evinces a prophetic self-understanding with the author. He may belong to a pious circle critical to the Hellenizing high priests around 170 BCE and knows that there is a group of righteous in Israel, with whom the divine judge will make peace and give them his protection and mercy. The coming judgment of God will lead to a universal re-creation. It is not clear whether "the righteous" also will include gentiles—this theme is covered in the next text from 1 En 10.

The poem about God's appearance as the end-time judge of the world, accompanied by his great army, the myriads of angels, draws on texts such as Deut 33:2; Hab 3:3–7, and Zech 14:5. God will also judge the Watchers, demonic figures who inflict sickness and evil on men.

Jesus' speech about the coming devastating war in Judea as a sign of the end-times suggests knowledge of 1 Enoch including this poetic vision (cf. Matt 24:30–31). And Jesus' woes against the rich (Luk 6:20–25; 16:1–8, 19–31) may be inspired by one of Enoch's exhortation speeches (1 En 94:6–11)—cf. e.g. 1 En 94:7–8 "Woe to those building their houses with iniquity, their foundations shall be destroyed, and they will fall by the sword. Those who amassed gold and silver shall perish instantly in the judgment. Woe to you who are rich, you put your trust in your wealth. From your riches you shall depart, for you did not remember the Most High in the days of your riches."

The nations shall bow down before the Lord

1 Enoch 10:16—11:1

Destroy all perversity from the face of the earth,
let every wicked deed be gone,
let the plant of righteousness appear:
it will become a blessing,
and the deeds of righteousness will be planted forever with joy.

All the righteous will escape,
and they will live until they beget thousands,
all the days of their youth and their old age will be completed in peace.
All the earth will be tilled in righteousness,
it will be planted with trees and filled with blessing,
trees of joy will be planted on it.
They will plant vines on it,
and every vine will yield a thousand measures,
each measure of olives will yield ten baths of oil.

Cleanse the earth from all impurity and all evil,
from all lawlessness and sin,
remove godlessness and impurities from the earth.
All the sons of men will become righteous,
all the nations will worship me,
all will prostrate themselves and bless me.

All the earth will be cleansed from defilement and uncleanness,
I shall nevermore send upon them any wrath or scourge.
I shall open the heavenly storehouses of blessing
and make them descend upon the earth,
upon the works and the labor of the sons of men.
Truth and peace will stand together
for all the days of eternity and all generations of men.

THIS PART OF 1 Enoch as well may be dated around the 170s BCE. The text is formulated as God's instructions to the archangel Michael to cleanse the earth from all evil. In this visionary text, God will renew the land and nation of Israel, using the pious remnant, "the plant of righteousness," as spearhead of the renewal. The perspective is then widened to the nations of the world, which will be cleansed and renewed and prostrate before the God of Israel. Then all the earth will experience the blessings of the new creation.

Neither this text nor the preceding from 1 En 1 mention any role for a messiah on earth. The heavenly actors are God and his archangel Michael, who see in mercy on the chosen ones on earth that will be the plant of righteousness.

The Lord of Heavens will descend to the earth

Book of Giants, 4Q530 2:13–20

The giants searched for one to explain to them the dream [. . .],
he told that Enoch, the scribe of distinction,
will interpret the dream for us.
Then Ohiyah, his brother confessed
and said in front of the giants:

I too had a frightening dream last night.
The Lord of heavens descended to the earth.
Thrones were set out
and the Great and Holy One took his seat.
Hundreds of angels served him,
thousands worshiped him,
all were standing before him.

And behold, scrolls were opened
and the judgment proclaimed.
The judgment was written in a scroll,
incised on a tablet—
a judgment on all living,
on all flesh and all powers.

This was my dream.

As the Lord once descended on Mt. Sinai, he will soon descend to judge heaven and earth. Even the evil spirits will be revealed that the time left for them is short. This throne scene belongs to the many visions of God's heavenly throne and the final judgment. The judge who is close at hand is God himself, as in Dan 7:9–10.

According to Gen 6:1–4, the giants are the offspring of the sons of God who brought iniquity to the earth and had intercourse with women (see above, p. 26). This dream vision belongs to the Enochic Book of Giants, written around the mid-second century BCE. According to this text, the giants are still around as evil spirits. One of them, Ohiyah, is here given a dream vision that elaborates how God will judge him, his peers, and all flesh. The text is inspired by Dan 7:7–9 and the poem that opens the Book of Watchers (pp. 142–43). To understand another dream vision, the giants need the help of Enoch, "the scribe of distinction"—Enoch acts as God's heavenly envoy to the giants.

The Book of Giants was in antiquity spread as no other Jewish book apart from the Bible. The Manicheans held it in high esteem; it was known from Syria to Mongolia and China. Five fragmentary copies of the original Aramaic text were found in Qumran.

On the Enochic Book of Giants, see pp. 215–16.

He shall cut off the scepter of evil

Sirach 35:20–26 (Cairo Geniza ms B)

The plea of the humble pierces the clouds,
it will not rest until it reaches its goal,
nor will he desist until the Most High responds,
acquits the righteous and delivers judgment.

Indeed, the Lord will not delay,
the Mighty will not hold back,
until he has crushed the loins of the merciless
and exacted vengeance on the nations,
before he has broken the scepter of the scoffer
and cut down the staff of evil.

He will repay every man according to his deeds,
judge the children of men according to their thoughts.
He will give his people justice
and make them rejoice in his deliverance.
His mercy is welcome in time of distress,
as clouds of rain are in time of drought.

The last two stanzas follow the Hebrew text, not the Greek of the Septuagint. Using the phrases "scepter of the scoffer" and "staff of evil," the author (or his later editor) sees a demonic power behind the nations that oppress Israel. When God gives his people justice and punishes the tyrannic nations, he will break the power of evil forever.

On Sir 35, see pp. 216–17.

The people of God will rise and make everything rest from the sword

4QApocryphon of Daniel, 4Q246 1–2

I.1 [fear] came [u]pon him. He fell before the throne of

2 [the king and said, "Live,] O king, forever! Wrath comes, and your years

3 [are counted. In] your vision [was revealed] everything that shall come forever.

4 [there will be b]attles, and oppression will come over the earth.

5 [There will be carnage in the land], and great slaughter in the provinces.

6 [All this will be brought about by] the king of Assyria. E]gypt

7 [will be ravaged and lie desolate This king] will be great on the earth,

8 [ ]all [the children of men will] worship and serve [him],

9 [ ] he shall call himself son of the g]reat [God], by his name he shall designate himself.

II.1 He shall call himself son of God, and they shall call him son of the Most High.

Like the meteors 2 that you saw, so shall their rule be changi[ng]:
they shall rule over the earth and trample everything down:

people shall trample upon people, province trample upon [pro]vince,

4 until the people of God will rise and make everything rest from the sword.

Its kingdom shall be an everlasting kingdom and all its paths in righteousness.

It shall jud[ge] the land in truth and make everything whole.

The sword shall cease from the earth, and all the provinces shall pay it homage.

The great God is its strength, he himself shall wage war for it.

He shall give peoples in its hand and cast them all down before it.

Its dominion shall be an everlasting dominion,

and all the depths of [Sheol will be subdued(?)]

ONLY A COLUMN AND a half has been preserved of this vision of present history and the end-times that will soon break in. In column 1, the beginning of the lines is missing (to make my partial restoration transparent I have kept the lines of this column).

A prophet-like person is called to the royal court to interpret the king's vision, as Joseph before pharaoh. The imaginary king is likely a Ptolemaic ruler in the early second century. The seer reveals that a blasphemous king will ravage the land of Egypt.

In the second century, the biblical term "king of Assyria" was reused about the ungodly king ruling from Syria, Antiochus Epiphanes, and Antiochus ravaged Egypt in his campaigns of 170–69. In the poem the king is portrayed as some kind of antichrist, who boasts of being the son of God. As in Dan 7:8, 11–12, the scoffing king will be judged by God and his rule terminated. The theme of the third stanza (2:1–3) is the continuing wars between the Ptolemies of Egypt and Seleucids of Syria through the third and early second centuries.

According to the fourth stanza, the people of God will stand forth as the victor on the world scene. As in Dan 7:15–27, God's elect servant on earth is no individual, no messiah, but the nation of God—we may talk about a collective messianism.

On 4Q246, the "Son of God-text," see pp. 217–19.

The earth will be like the Garden of Eden

Renewed Earth, 4Q475

He chose [Zio]n, and [expected] a righteous life [. . .]
But they forgot his precepts and did not seek them,
and [polluted] the [precious] land.
[He stretched out his h]ands in their midst,
and told them all [his commandments].
A]ll the earth [he will renew],
there will no longer be any guilt in the land,
iniquity will not b[e any more].
[After destruc]tion and great wrath,
all the earth will be like the Garden of Eden,
and all who li[ve there shall flourish,]
The land will be have peace forever,
those who live there will seek [his torah.]
[Israel will be unto Him] a beloved son,
they will seek all [his ways,]
and ri[ghteousness will unfold in his nation.]

THIS NINE-LINE FRAGMENT PRESERVES a part of a visionary Qumran poem on the end-times. Even if the nation of Israel failed, God will renew both the land of Israel and all the earth. Israel will be to him a beloved son, and the earth will be like the Garden of Eden.

The Hebrew word *'arets* can mean both "the land" (of Israel) and "the earth"—in each case the interpreter or translator must make his choice. The fragment fared badly, both margins had decayed, but we sense the poetic power of the text. As official editor of this text I tried to restore the meaning of the poem through simple restorations.

Smite the nations who fight against you

War Scroll, 1QM 12:2–16

With the graving-tool of life you engraved the names of all their hosts—
the book is with you in your holy dwelling—
yeah, the names of the righteous,
with whom you made your covenant of peace in your great mercy,
to rule over them forever and ever.

You muster the armies of your elect ones, in their thousands,
with all your holy angels, to direct them in battle
so that they may smite the rebels of the earth by your great judgments,
and prevail together with the elect of heaven.

You are an awesome God in the splendor of your majesty,
the community of your holy angels is in our midst
to support us through all the ages.

Kings we will despise, the mighty we will mock,
for our Lord is holy, the King of Glory is with us.
The nation of his holy ones are our heroes,
the army of his angels is enlisted with us,
the valiant angel of war is among us,
the army of his spirits follow our steps.
Our horsemen are like clouds and dew covering the earth,
as showers of rain shedding judgment on all her offspring.

Rise up, O hero!
Lead off your captives, O glorious one!
Gather up your spoils, O valiant fighter!
Lay your hand on the neck of your enemies,
your feet on the pile of the slain!
Smite the nations who fight against you,
devour the flesh of the sinner with your sword!

Fill your land with glory,
your inheritance with blessing,
let there be an abundance of cattle in your fields,
silver, gold, and precious stones in your palaces.

Rejoice greatly, O Zion,
Shine with jubilation, Jerusalem.
Rejoice, all you cities of Judah,
keep your gates open forever
that the wealth of the nations may be brought in.

Their kings shall serve you,
their oppressors shall bow down before you,
they shall lick the dust of your feet.
Shout for joy, daughters of my people,
deck yourselves with glorious jewels,
and rule over the kingdoms of the nations,
[. . .] so that Israel may rule forever.

The hymn has biblical roots: God will punish enemy nations that have oppressed Israel and give his people victory and blessing. Evil forces support the sons of darkness, while the angels join ranks with the sons of light.

This is the most militant and nationalistic among the songs about the last days included here. The War Scroll was found in possibly seven copies in the Qumran caves. The book is the blueprint of the Qumranite Union for the end-time war, where the sons of light fight against the sons of darkness. First, the community will defeat its enemies within the people of Israel, restore the temple and the sacrificial cult. Subsequently the gentiles who have inflicted evil on Israel will be beaten down by God's armies. The Lord's armies are the troops of the community, with officers, soldiers, and field chaplains who bless the troops, knowing that the sons of light are partaking in the fight of the heavenly angels against the powers of evil.

On the War Scroll, see pp. 219–21.

The time of righteousness has come

4QTime of Righteousness, 4Q215a

[They will pass through affliction,]
tribulations by the hand of the oppressor,
and see the trials of the pit.
Through this they shall be refined
and become the elect of righteousness,
all their sins shall be wiped out
because of his loving kindness.

For the period of wickedness has been completed
and all injustice will have an end.
For the time of righteousness has come,
the land has been filled with knowledge of God
and glorification of him in [his be]auty.
For the age of peace has come
with the laws of truth and testimony of justice,
to instruct [every man] in the ways of God
and his mighty deeds [and knowledge of him] forever.

Every tongue shall bless him,
every man shall bow down before him,
[and they will be] of on[e hea]rt.
For he knew their recompense before they were created,

and assigned the borders [and times] of the deeds of righteousness
through all generations.

For the dominion of good has come,
the throne [of righteousness] has been elevated,
knowledge, prudence, and insight are raised high.
Tested by [his] holy plan are the men of humility,
[the elect of truth].

THE FRAGMENTS OF THIS scroll were given the name "Time of Righteousness." This visionary text moves from creation to the world to come. The text above could represent the end of the scroll: God will create all things anew, and all mankind will partake in the age of redemption. Every tribe and tongue will share in the praise of God and prostrate before him. The scroll was copied some decades before the turn of the era, the text itself may go back to the second century BCE.

On 4QTime of Righteousness, see p. 221.

List of Source Texts

11QPsalms[a] 26. Praise to him who created the earth by his might.

4Q403 Songs of the Sabbath Sacrifice frg. 1 1:30–43. Heavenly singers, give him honor and praise.

1QS Community Rule 10:8–18. My lips play flute after his guiding line.

1QH[a] Thanksgiving Hymns 19:3–14. You enlighten me about your wondrous deeds.

4Q434 Barkhi Nafshi frg. 1:1–13. He circumcised the foreskin of our hearts.

Wisdom of Solomon 11:20–26. You love all the living.

1 Enoch 84:2–6. Enoch's prayer.

Jubilees 10:3–6. Noah's prayer.

Jubilees 12:19–20. Abraham's prayer.

1Q34 Festival Prayers frg. 3, 2:5–8. You renewed your covenant with us.

4Q504 Words of the Luminaries[a] frgs. 1–2 5:2—6:16. Look to us in our trials.

Psalms of Solomon 7. Do not turn us over to the nations.

Psalms of Solomon 9. You cast us out of the land you gave us.

Judith 9:7–12, 14. Save us from the Assyrians.

2 Maccabees 1:24–29. Gather your dispersed people.

2 Maccabees 15:21–24. Not by force of arms.

Sirach 36:13–19. Let Zion be filled with songs of praise.

Tobit 13:9–17. The towers of Jerusalem shall be built in gold.

11QPsalms[a] 22. Zion shall be honored all over the earth.

Psalms of Solomon 11. The Lord gathers his children from East and West.

Psalms of Solomon 5. You give nourishment to all the living.

Psalms of Solomon 16. I fell asleep and came close to dying.

4Q525 Wisdom text frg. 1 1–3, frg. 2 2:1–7. Blessed is the man who has a pure heart.

Psalms of Solomon 6. Blessed is he who calls on the name of the Lord.

Sirach 51:1–12. I called on my Father and he saved me from death.

Joseph and Aseneth 12:5—13:15. You are Father for the orphan.

Prayer of Manasseh. You receive the penitent one.

Sirach 51:13–19/11QPs[a] 21:11–17. Burning for God's Wisdom.

1QH[a] Thanksgiving Hymns 10:5–21. You opened in me a fountain of knowledge.

1QH[a] Thanksgiving Hymns 15:29–36. You taught me wisdom by your truth.

1QH[a] Thanksgiving Hymns 9:23–39. You opened my ear to wondrous mysteries.

1QH[a] Thanksgiving Hymns 6:19–33. You make me jealous for your ways.

1QS Community Rule 11:2–20. My eyes have gazed at eternal mysteries.

Sirach 24:30–34. I am a source watering the garden.

Ps 151A/11QPs[a] 151:3–12. He set me as prince of his people.

1 Maccabees 3:3–9. Judah the Maccabee, the Lion of Judah.

1 Maccabees 14:4–15. Prince Simon made peace in the land.

4Q448 Apocryphal Psalm and Prayer 2–3. Blessing upon a Hasmonean King.

Psalms of Solomon 17:4–9, 20–26. Raise up their king, the son of David.

4Q521 Messianic apocalypse frg. 2 2:1–13. Heaven and earth will obey his messiah.

1QSa Messianic Rule 2:11–22. The end-time priest and the end-time prince.

1QSb Rule of Blessings 5:20–28. You judge the nations by the power of your mouth.

1QSb Rule of Blessings 3:22–28, 4:22–28. May you be like an angel serving in his holy habitation.

4Q541 Levi apocryph frg. 9 1:1–7. He shall atone for the children of his generation.

4Q491c. War text. God has enthroned me in the heavenly council.

Testament of Levi 18. His star shall rise in heaven.

11QMelchizedek 2:4–25. Melchizedek—the heavenly redeemer.

1 Enoch 1:3–9. God will descend and judge the world.

1 Enoch 10:16—11:1. The nations shall bow down before the Lord.

4Q530 Enoch and the Giants[b] 2:16–20. The Lord of Heavens will descend to the earth.

Sirach 35:20–26. He shall cut off the scepter of evil.

4Q246 Pseudo-Daniel 1–2. The people of God will rise and make everything rest from the sword.

4Q475 Renewed Earth. The earth will be like the Garden of Eden.

1QM War Scroll 12:2–16. Smite the nations who fight against you.

4Q215a Time of Righteousness. The Time of righteousness has come.

Introduction to the Source Texts

In this section follows historical-literary introductions to the source books or source texts. The first time a source book is represented in the collection, the book as such will be introduced here. Should another poem from the same source book appear later, it may be followed by comments also then. This section will, for interested readers, serve as an introduction to essential parts of late Second Temple Jewish literature.

11QPsalms[a]

pp. 3–4, 53–54, 79–80.

Qumran scrolls are designated by the number of the cave in which the scroll was found followed by Q, for Qumran. Scrolls were found—by the Bedouin and archaeologists—in eleven of the many caves surrounding Qumran between 1947 and 1956. This text is designated 11QPs[a]Creat, Hymn to the Creator.

The Bedouin discovered Cave 11, 3 kilometers north of Qumran, in 1956. 11QPs[a] is the largest preserved psalm scroll from the Judean Desert. Remnants of thirty-four psalm scrolls were found in Qumran, and two more were left by the Zealots at Masada. Some of these "psalm scrolls" contained only a few of the biblical psalms, and none would include all 150 psalms of the biblical Psalter—such a scroll would be too large and impractical to handle.

When this scroll came into the hands of scholars, it appeared as a bundle, and the innermost layers were impossible to unroll. In 1961, when the young scholar James A. Sanders started to study the scroll, he was advised to use a humidifier to soften these layers. On one of his first days at the Rockefeller Museum, he left the bundle with the inner layers directly above the humidifier and walked out for lunch. In hindsight we would judge this irresponsible handling of an antique artifact—but returning an hour and a half later, he found that these layers could be unrolled relatively easily and subsequently read.

The scroll contained thirty-two of the biblical psalms (from Ps 101 to 150, but not in sequence) plus eight psalms from outside the Psalter of the Hebrew Bible. Four of them were known from before:

- One is Ps 151, known from the Septuagint, the Greek translation of the Bible.
- Two more have been included among five "extra psalms" in some Syriac versions of the Bible, there numbered Pss 154 and 155.
- One is known from the book of Sirach ("Burning for God's Wisdom," p. 79).

Of the four "new psalms," three are included in this book—the next one is the hymn to Zion on pp. 53–54. The end of 11QPs[a] is formatted with a Davidic-messianic edge. "David's last words" (2 Sam 21:1–7) is followed by "David's compositions" and Ps 140, with the last column containing Ps 134:1–3 and two biographical David-psalms known from the Septuagint: Ps 151A and 151B. "David's Compositions" is a résumé-like list of publications ascribed to King David, covering the entire liturgical year—a list likely originating in the Qumran movement.

The character of this scroll has been intensely debated: (1) was it regarded as a biblical scroll, demonstrating that the shape of the Davidic Psalter was open and flexible until the early first century CE, or (2) was it simply a "hymnbook," i.e., a liturgical scroll? Scholars supporting the first option assert that Pss 1–89 had grown to a stable unit around 100 BCE, while the full Davidic Psalter reached its final form only some years after the turn of the era. This author supports the second option. Psalms 1–151 were translated into Greek early in the first century BCE in Egypt—demonstrating that the shape of the Psalter was fixed around 100 BCE, after a steady literary growth from the fifth to the second century.

Scrolls made for liturgical use could include biblical psalms as well as other texts. The script of 11QPs[a] can be dated to the first half of the first century CE, but the collection is probably of an earlier date—this specific hymnal is also represented by a scroll from Cave 4, 4Q88. And this is only one of the hymnals used by the Qumranite Union, which had separate liturgies for festivals, for the Sabbath sacrifices, and for morning and evening prayers, and used the Thanksgiving Hymns as a book of prayer.

Apart from the résumé-like "David's list of publications," the nonbiblical psalms were likely composed during the third and second centuries. Some may have been sung by the Levites in the temple before the Essenes broke with the Hasmonean establishment—a schism I date to around 140 BCE.

In style, the Hymn to the Creator can be compared with biblical psalms. God is portrayed seated on his throne, surrounded by his heavenly entourage. He marches forth surrounded by his angels and his glory—this can be compared with the biblical theophanies in Deut 33:2; Judg 5:4–5; and Hab 3:3. The angels appear as the applauding audience during the act of creation—a feature not found in Genesis 1 (but perhaps presupposed in the words "Let us create man in our image" [v. 26]). God's glorious presence and the "tumult of many waters" point to Ezekiel's throne vision in Ezek 1–2.

Genesis 1 speaks about God's spirit and creative word. As the Hymn to the Creator has it, God used his might, wisdom, understanding, and heart-knowledge in the act of creation. But God's creation is not limited to a one-time act in the beginning. The Creator is still at work, giving nourishment to all the living, as described in Ps 104.

Revelation 1:9–20 describes the risen Christ in a similar fashion to the enthroned Creator in this psalm. According to John 1:1–5, Christ is the creative Word, God's agent in the act of creation (cf. the role of Lady Wisdom in Prov 8:22–31). In the New

Testament we find visions of God's throne in Acts 7:55–60 and Rev 4–5. Another throne vision appears in the Enochic book of Giants (see pp. 147–48).

Songs of the Sabbath Sacrifice

pp. 5–7.

Songs of the Sabbath Sacrifice are preserved in nine (incomplete) manuscripts from Qumran and in one from Masada—I surmise that Essenes fled from Qumran when the Roman armies approached Jericho in June 68, joining the Zealot group that had taken over the Herodian fortress Masada.

Each scroll originally contained liturgies for thirteen consecutive Sabbaths, possibly to be recited during the first four months of the year, in springtime and early summer.

We might ask whether the songs were written and collected by the Essenes or had already been compiled before them. Unfortunately, there is no scholarly consensus about this. In the songs we do not perceive any contrast between righteous singers on earth and other ungodly Israelites, as we do in other Qumranite texts. There is no trace of the strong disagreements between Essene thinkers and the temple establishment. But these songs represent another genre from the clearly Qumranite texts, so the scribes might have expressed themselves differently here.

It is pertinent here to explain my use of the terms "Qumranite" and "Qumran movement." Sometime in the first century BCE, an Essene subgroup settled at the site we call Qumran. Following archaeologist Jodi Magness, most scholars hold that the Essenes arrived around 90 BCE. Alternatively, during the 30s, the early years of Herod, a Hasmonean settlement from the 80s was taken over by Essenes (like Joan Taylor and the archaeologist Jean-Baptiste Humbert, I sympathize with this view.) These settlers belonged to an elite group within the larger Essene movement that called themselves the "Union" (*Yahad*)—in this book I use the terms "Qumran movement" more widely and "Union," "Qumran Community," and "Qumranite" more narrowly. Perhaps fifty to sixty members of the Union lived at Qumran, most of them dwelling in nearby caves.

The present version of the songs reflects editing in the Qumran movement after the Essenes parted from the Hasmonean elite and the priests that supported them in the early Hasmonean period. Each song opens with the term "for the Master," and the title Master/Instructor (*maskil*) designates the leader of the Qumran community. However, I think it likely that the main body of this liturgy is pre-Essene and goes back to the Levitical choir that performed in the temple in early Maccabean times. The idea of union between earthly and the heavenly communities perceived in these songs was common in temple theology and so was carried on by the Essenes. The scribes of the Qumran movement knew that their community on earth was allied with the angels of heaven. The singers of the spiritual temple sensed a spiritual connection with their heavenly counterparts and could participate in the praises within the heavenly sanctuary.

In Exod 25:40, Moses is told to build the tabernacle "according to the image shown to you on the mountain." In the second century BCE, this verse comes to be interpreted as a vision of the heavenly sanctuary; it is the blueprint for the tabernacle, so it is no wonder that there is harmony between the singers of the heavenly temple and their earthly counterparts.

The heavenly temple would become an important theme for pious ones in Israel. In the New Testament this theme permeates the Letter to the Hebrews and the book of Revelation. In some later writings (rabbinic and extrarabbinic), the *merkavah*, God's heavenly chariot, would become an object of reflection and awe. Thus, there are thematic lines from the Songs of the Sabbath Sacrifice to these early mystical traditions.

The Community Rule

pp. 8–11, 94–97.

The Community Rule is the central rule book of the Qumran community, a rule book that underwent literary growth and existed in different recensions. The longest version is the beautiful "library copy" from Cave 1, 185 centimeters long with eleven columns. When the Bedouin came into the cave in 1947, the scroll was deposited in the same jar as the Great Isaiah Scroll.

The skin in the first half of the Great Isaiah Scroll (chapters 1–33) has the same mineral features as the Community Rule. These two rolls were processed at the same time in a workshop in Judea, a workshop that used the ancient world's most advanced techniques for producing and providing parchment rolls to skilled scribes. In the processing workshop, the skin was lightly tanned and treated with "mineral juices" with ingredients such as sulfur, potassium, calcium, calium, silicium, magnesium, and aluminium sulfate—and the smooth side of the skin prepared for inscribing was treated slightly differently from the back side.

Ten copies of the same rule tradition were found in Cave 4 and one in Cave 5, and there are literary differences between them. A late copy, $4QS^d$ from 30–1 BCE, represents the shortest text, containing material parallel to 1QS 5–10. Most scholars nevertheless regard the shorter edition as the earliest core and see a gradual process of literary growth toward the larger literary edition of 1QS around 100 BCE. This literary growth did allow for continued variation in the contents of various rule scrolls. 1QS incorporates material not found in the other copies, such as the yearly liturgy of covenant renewal (1:16—2:26) and a treatise on the spirits of light and darkness that govern the ways of men (3:13—5:17).

For the settlers living at Qumran, the prescriptions of the Community Rule were essential. The Rule does not contain prescriptions relating to family life. Were only men living here? The adjacent graveyard contains around a thousand graves. A few dozen graves have been excavated, and a few skeletons were confirmed to be from females. Some scholars suggest that most of the year only men resided at this scribal center, possibly due to the scribal character of the settlement or to strict purity rules governing relations between the sexes. The excavator of the Qumran settlement Roland de Vaux compared the community with early Christian monasticism—and we may note that de Vaux, a biblical scholar and archaeologist, also was a Catholic cleric.

However, the Union was also represented among Essenes elsewhere in Judea; some texts originating in the Qumranite Union presuppose family life and regular business relations with outsiders, and Josephus sets the number of male Essenes at four thousand (compared to six thousand Pharisees). Of the approximately five hundred literary works represented by the 950 more or less fragmentary scrolls found in the Qumran caves, perhaps one hundred and fifty were authored by members of the Union. (Scholars recognize organizational features characteristic of the Union, terms typical of their theology and literary tradition, and specific orthographic features, all of which I call "Qumranite.")

Before its destruction by the elements of nature, the Qumranite library would have included more than a thousand scrolls. It remains an enigma how the Essene scribal center at Qumran could have one thousand book scrolls at their disposal—a huge fortune in those days. Some of the scrolls were written on parchment of remarkably high quality, such as the Temple Scroll from Cave 11, and the Great Isaiah Scroll and the Community Rule—both stored in the same jar in Cave 1.

The Essene Union parted from the temple establishment around the mid-second century BCE. Priests with leadership offices in the Union had an intimate knowledge of the temple milieu. Further, many Qumran writings have been classified by scholars as "pre-Qumranic" or "extra-Qumranic." Thus, Essene scribes, including scribes residing at Qumran, had at their disposal scrolls originating in other milieus from early Hasmonean times and onwards.

Some of the Qumran liturgies reflect the narrow theology of the Union, while others preserve traditions from the temple or from Judea at large. The Union may be the first group prescribing daily individual prayer in Jewish tradition. The prayers in columns 10–11 of the Community Rule have the liturgical daily prayers as a central point of reference.

Lim, Timothy H. *The Dead Sea Scrolls. A Very Short Introduction.* Very Short Introductions. Oxford: Oxford University Press, 2017.

Perrin, Andrew B. *Lost Words and Forgotten Worlds of the Dead Sea Scrolls.* Lexham, UK: Lexham, forthcoming.

The Thanksgiving Hymns

pp. 12–13, 83–93.

The Thanksgiving Hymns (*Hodayot*) is a central prayer book of the Qumran community. There were two copies of this work in Cave 1 (of 1QHodayot[b] only one substantial fragment was preserved) and six in Cave 4 (the largest scroll depository of the community). Most of twenty-eight columns were preserved in the large scroll from Cave 1, which has served as the basis for a reconstruction of the scroll and deciphering of its text, which could be supplemented by text preserved in the copies from Cave 4.

The hymns may be traced back to early Essene circles from the second half of the second century BCE onwards—while the earliest of the Cave 4 copies was penned in the mid-first century BCE. Most psalms open with the words "I thank you, God." These psalms are a primary source of our knowledge of the "Qumranic soul," the inside of Essene piety. They reveal a community intensely aware of their own sinfulness, contrasted with God's sovereignty. The singers know that they have been raised from dust and elected to be God's true sons, children of his mercy. There are many parallels to ideas and terms from the New Testament.

The first nine columns of the 1QH[a] scroll contain community songs in praise of God. Then follow eight columns with "Teacher Hymns," where the (imagined) singer is a teacher who has experienced suffering and is a source of revelation and blessings for his community; these are followed by more community hymns.

For Further Reading

Harkins, Angela Kim. "Hodayot (H)." In *T. & T. Clark Companion to the Dead Sea Scrolls*, edited by George J. Brooke and Charlotte Hempel, 314–18. T. & T. Clark Companions. London: T. & T. Clark, 2019.

Schuller, Eileen M., and Carol A. Newsom. *The Hodayot (Thanksgiving Psalms): A Study Edition of 1QH^a^*. Early Judaism and Its Literature 36. Atlanta: SBL, 2012.

Barkhi Nafshi

pp. 15–17.

The hymnic collection Barkhi Nafshi ("Bless, my soul") was found in five fragmentary copies in Qumran Cave 4 (4Q434–438). Many of the hymns opened with "Bless the Lord, O my soul." Typical for early Jewish psalmody, the hymns are steeped in language and imagery of biblical texts, in particular from the Psalms, Isaiah, and Jeremiah. Body images and metaphors symbolize spiritual responsiveness: eyes, ears, tongue, lips, neck, heart, hands, foreskin, and feet. We do not find here terms typical of the Qumranite Union, so these psalms likely represent a wider Judean tradition. The predominant threat is from gentiles and the evil inclination; there is no cosmic fight against Belial and the sons of darkness. However, many aspects of the hymns would resonate with Qumranite piety. Reciting the hymns, members of the Union would reinforce their conviction of belonging to God's end-time elect community.

For Further Reading

Falk, Daniel K. "Barkhi Nafshi." In *T. & T. Clark Companion to the Dead Sea Scrolls*, edited by George J. Brooke and Charlotte Hempel, 286–88. T. & T. Clark Companions. London: T. & T. Clark, 2019.

Wisdom of Solomon

pp. 18–19.

The Old Testament Apocrypha (or the deuterocanonical writings) is a Christian collection of Jewish writings from the last two centuries before the turn of the era, primarily written in Hebrew and Aramaic. These books were not included in the Jewish Bible when its "table of contents" was finally decided in the second century CE, although Sirach was probably considered a borderline case. With time, most of these books were forgotten in the synagogue and transmitted in their Greek form. We do not know who translated the books into Greek; some translators may have been Jewish Christians who in part functioned as a kind of bridge between the people of Israel and the church, which with time became more and more gentile. In their Greek form these books were read and transmitted in the church, not least in monasteries; the same was the case with the so-called Old Testament Pseudepigrapha.The three earliest Christian Bibles we know were inscribed and bound around 400 CE—Vaticanus, Alexandrinus, and Sinaiticus. In addition to the books of the Hebrew Bible, they included these other Jewish writings, not in the same literary sequence and with some differences in their "tables of contents." These Jewish writings were popular in the churches and deemed worthy of inclusion in the biblical codex. Today they are usually included in Catholic and Orthodox editions of the Bible.

The Wisdom of Solomon or Book of Wisdom is the latest of the deuterocanonical books, and among the few written in Greek. It was penned in Egypt by the mid-first century BCE, most likely in Alexandria, which had a large Jewish population.

In chapters 1–6 and 11–19, the book presents itself as a parenetic book on wisdom from above and on the ways of the righteous and the ungodly, with chapters 11–19 containing admonitions based on exegesis of Exodus and Numbers. "Hiding" under the name of Solomon, the book asserts to be a continuation of his legendary wisdom.

Lady Wisdom, residing at God's side (cf. Prov 1–9), is portrayed in 1:4, 6:12–24, and 7:21—11:4. She is a personified divine attribute that represents God's action in the world. She was there from the beginning, witnessing the act of creation. The righteous are exhorted to partner with divine Wisdom and follow her advice. As she does in Sirach, so here too personified Wisdom has a special relationship to the nation of Israel. Biblical sages exemplify how God and his Wisdom have protected and guided the elect ones of Israel.

Following the exhortation to kings in 6:1–21, King Solomon enters the scene (without being explicitly named). Chapters 7–10 praise Wisdom and in a more hidden sense also King Solomon. Chapter 8 employs language that recalls the sensuality of the love poem to Lady Wisdom in Sir 51 (pp. 79–80, 199–200) and the poems of the Song of Songs, which probably were written in the same century as the Wisdom of Solomon. The search for wisdom by the righteous is described as follows: "I sought her from my youth; I fell in love with her beauty. I desired to take her for my bride and became enamored of her beauty" (8:2).

The author encourages his fellow Jews in the diaspora to endure times of hardship (2:12–20; 19:13–16) and to hold firm to the faith of Israel when they reside in a Hellenistic, pagan culture. However, the Wisdom of Solomon also reflects Judaism's encounter with Hellenism. As Stoic philosophers spoke about logos (Word) as the unifying element of the universe, so the book portrays Wisdom as reaching from one end of the earth to the other and penetrating all things (7:24; 8:1). Furthermore, in Greek thinking, the soul exists before the body and is burdened by it; these ideas also appear in the Wisdom of Solomon (8:19–20; 9:15).

Without its superscription, the full book does not present itself as originating with Solomon: it does not open with his name or with allusions to him as do Proverbs and the final recension of the Song of Songs. The "royal chapters" of the book (6–9, 11) bridge the instruction of chapters 1–5 and the midrashic exhortation of chapters 11–19. With its admonition to walk with Lady Wisdom and with chapters devoted to Solomon, the book easily invites a superscription that makes Solomon its originator. However, we do not know how early the superscription "Wisdom of Solomon" was added; it is present with slight variations in the Septuagint codices.

For Further Reading

Short introductions to each book of the Old Testament Apocrypha are found in *The SBL Study Bible. New Revised Standard Version. Updated Edition, with the Apocryphal/Deuterocanonical Books.* New York: HarperOne, 2023.

For more comprehensive introductions, see:

DeSilva, David A. *Introducing the Apocrypha: Message, Context, and Significance.* 2nd ed. Grand Rapids: Baker Academic, 2018.

Wills, Lawrence M. *Introduction to the Apocrypha: Jewish Books in Christian Bibles.* New Haven: Yale University Press, 2021.

For a general introduction to the Pseudepigrapha, see the Introduction by Richard Bauckham and James R. Davila in *Old Testament Pseudepigrapha: More Noncanonical Scriptures*, edited by Richard Bauckham, et al., 1:xii–xxxviii. 2 vols. Grand Rapids: Eerdmans, 2013.

1 Enoch

pp. 23–24, 142–46.

First Enoch, a collection of four books oriented toward the end-time, grew together during the second century BCE. The first part, the Book of Watchers (chapters 1–36) has roots back to the third century. The poem that introduces the Book of Watchers, about God revealing himself on the Day of Judgment, is rendered on pp. 142–43. Sometime after the turn of the era another book was added, the Parables of chapters 37–71.

In the Book of Watchers and the Parables, Enoch, the sage from Gen 5 who was taken up to God, receives a tour of the heavenly regions with an angelic guide. He receives a revelation that he, in this critical time for Israel, will pass on to righteous listeners on earth. Here we sense spiritual "disciples of Enoch," some of whom perhaps imagined themselves spiritually connected with their heavenly ideal, and then writing down books in his name. Enoch is told that God will judge heaven and earth and renew the world.

Towards the end of the collection, Israel's history is retold in allegorical form (the Dream Visions, chapters 83–90); this is followed by Exhortation Speeches (chapters 91–105). In the latter, the short Animal Apocalypse is editorially included (93:1–10; 91:11–17). The allegory signals that God will lead the nation through trials to freedom and peace. The righteous in the nation are thus admonished to keep up faith and hope.

For the circles behind the Enochic books, these texts are divinely inspired and contain instruction as important as that in the recognized books of Scripture. In the first centuries after the turn of the era, many Jews and Christians believed that Enoch indeed had authored these books, which therefore contained inspired revelation. Some New Testament authors quote or refer to the Book of Watchers as an authority (see Matt 24; 1–2 Peter; and Jude).

Despite its popularity, the rabbis did not include 1 Enoch when the borders of the Tanakh, the Jewish Bible, were drawn in the second century CE. In contrast, there were church fathers who valued 1 Enoch highly. Tertullian argued against rabbis who said that Enoch could not have written the book, as any book written by him would not have survived the flood. For Tertullian, Noah could have kept the book of his great-grandfather in the ark, or he could have reconstructed it through the inspiration of the Spirit. In contrast, Augustine held that no books written so early could have survived, so books carrying the names of Enoch and Noah could not have been written by them and should have no place in the canon.

The Enochic books were written in Aramaic. Seven fragmentary Qumran scrolls contain parts of 1 Enoch in an early form.

With or without the later Parables, the collection was subsequently translated into Greek. Sometime between the fourth and the sixth century, the complete book of Enoch was translated from Greek into Ethiopic (into Geez, a Semitic language) as part of translating the Bible into Ethiopic—from 340 CE, Axum with its bishop was the center of Ethiopic Christianity, with close links to Coptic and West Syrian tradition. The full text of 1 Enoch is extant only in Ethiopic, in more than 120 manuscripts from the fourteenth century onwards, but parts of it are preserved in two different Greek recensions. The Aramaic Qumran fragments confirm that the text was polished and received editorial changes during its odyssey from Aramaic through Greek to Ethiopic. The Parables are known to us only from the Ethiopic Bible. First Enoch is generally reckoned as one of the Old Testament Pseudepigrapha.

The books of Enoch belong to Jewish apocalyptic literature—among its "cousins" we find Daniel and the Testaments of the Twelve Patriarchs. In books written in the apocalyptic genre, an interpreting angel reveals secrets about present and future events to a sage on earth. These writings continue two lines of tradition from the Bible: they may be seen as a crossbreed of sapiential scribal tradition and prophetic self-consciousness. In the encounter with threatening empires and in times of crisis during the period from 250 to 60 BCE, these writings proclaimed hope and faith in the God of history. Ungodly empires will pass away and give way to a time of salvation that God will inaugurate for Israel and other nations, with his faithful community on earth as the elect core.

The book of Revelation represents an analogous prophetic-apocalyptic response to another time of crisis, with Nero and the Roman Empire inflicting evil on both Jews and Christians. Books that do not display the characteristics of apocalypse can nevertheless share with that genre a similar worldview. This is true of many writings from Qumran.

The Book of Jubilees

pp. 25–27.

In its complete form, Jubilees is known only in Ethiopic, as part of the Ethiopic Bible, and additionally in fragmentary Greek manuscripts. With 1 Enoch it was translated from Greek into Ethiopic between the fourth and sixth centuries CE, as part of the larger project of translating the Bible into Ethiopic.

Eighteen Qumran manuscripts preserve parts of Jubilees. There are differences between the Hebrew texts from around the turn of the era and the Ethiopic texts, preserved in manuscripts from the fourteenth century onwards. The Qumran texts show that the book was composed in Hebrew, and it would necessarily undergo changes during its odyssey from Hebrew through Greek to Ethiopic. Only one of the Qumran manuscripts bears features that suggest it could have contained all of Jubilees (4Q223–224).

Based on its contents, earlier scholars suggested that the book was composed in Judea around 160 BCE, either written as a whole or in two stages, where a later editor substantively expanded the earlier version. They usually asserted that the Hebrew version would have looked much like the later Ethiopic text.

A recent scholar (Matthew Monger) has shown, however, that only the creation story is present in the earliest manuscript, penned around 100 BCE (Jub 2:1–4, 7–24). He argues for a gradually literal growth of the book throughout the first century BCE, in circles either within or close to the Qumran movement.[1]

The introduction to Jubilees recalls that God on Mount Sinai told Moses that the nation of Israel would turn from their God, while a small, pious remnant would seek him with all their heart and submit to God's commandments as they were prescribed; here we sense a hidden "prophecy" about the first-century circle of authors. Subsequently, God's angel would dictate to Moses an expanded version of the biblical storyline from creation to the exodus from Egypt—as we now have it in Jubilees. Already in the retelling of Genesis, we sense the authors' "right understanding"

1. Monger, "Many Forms of Jubilees."

of Israel's festival calendar, with months, years, and Jubilee Years (hence the book's title, Jubilees). This understanding of the Torah was thus authorized by the highest authority! In this version of the patriarchal stories, the fathers follow the festival calendar later revealed to Moses. For the authors, who probably were connected to priestly circles, it is essential that all the nation follow strict purity rules.

The second stanza of Noah's prayer mentions "the watchers," the fallen angels. This refers to the story in Gen 6:1–4, about the sons of God who brought sin and iniquity to the earth. In the Bible, the term "sons of God" usually refers to the angels, and Gen 6:1–4 is commonly interpreted as referencing angels who turned from God. Some texts from the second and first centuries BCE assert that the offspring of these fallen angels, "the watchers," became evil spirits who want to inflict evil on humanity. In the Book of Watchers (the first part of 1 Enoch), Enoch is portrayed as the mediator between God and the watchers: he brings God's judgment upon their knowledge. Another Enochic book, the Book of Giants, is known from seven fragmentary Qumran manuscripts and from later Manichean tradition (see p. 147–48, 215–16).

Noah prays that God, in his mercy, will see to his offspring—in particular to "the sons of righteousness" within Israel, guarding them against influence from evil spirits, and giving them his blessings.

For Further Reading

Monger, Matthew. "The Many Forms of Jubilees: A Reassessment of the Manuscript Evidence from Qumran and the Lines of Transmission of the Parts and Whole of Jubilees." *Revue de Qumran* 30 (2018) 191–211.

———. "4Q216—A New Material Analysis." *Semitica* 60 (2018) 309–33.

VanderKam, James C. *Jubilees: The Hermeneia Translation*. Hermeneia. Minneapolis: Fortress, 2020.

Jubilees and the Story of Abraham and the Idols

p. 27.

Both Jewish and Muslim traditions recall that the young Abraham renounced the idols that his father, Terah, and his larger family worshiped. Early on he understood that there is one true God that cannot be portrayed by an image or idol. Jubilees is the earliest literary reference to this motif. In this episode Abraham has arrived with his close family in the land of Haran. He has learned that the stars would foretell how the crops will do in the coming year. When the new moon inaugurates the seventh month he looks up to heaven and understands that stars and heavenly bodies are in the hands of God—it must be God and not the stars who decides about rain and the crops in their seasons.

Here we encounter the idea that the first day in the seventh month is a day of destiny for the year to follow. In the Hebrew Bible this is a minor festival day, the day of blowing the ram's horn, the shofar (Lev 23:24–25; Num 29:1–6). From the time of the book of Jubilees onwards this day grew in importance, and with time it would be celebrated as the Jewish New Year, Rosh Hashanah. On this day God not only decides about rain and crops but also determines the destiny of humans and nations for the year to come, and possibly forever.

On this day Abraham confesses his faith and confidence in the one God and asks for his help and protection, for himself and his seed, which will become the people of Israel. Here the storyline of Jubilees comes to the transition between chapters 11 and 12 in Genesis. As an answer to Abraham's prayer and confession, God begins to reveal himself to him, telling him to go to a land God will show him (Gen 12:1–3).

Festival Prayers from Qumran

pp. 28–29.

In Qumran scrolls one finds liturgical prayers for each day of the week, and others for Ssabbaths and festivals. Columns 2–3 of the

Community Rule describe a yearly rite of covenant renewal, to be celebrated during the Feast of Weeks. This prayer seems to be at home in this setting.

Many Qumran liturgies are not marked by the narrow traditionalist views of the Essene Union. Some of these texts preserve liturgical traditions from early Hasmonean times, perhaps from a milieu close to the temple, and later slightly adapted by priests in the Qumran movement. This goes for Words of the Luminaries—prayers for each day of the week (4Q504, 4Q506, pp. 30–32) and Barkhi Nafshi ("Bless, my soul," 4Q434–438, pp. 15–17). Words of the Luminaries and Festival Prayers (1Q34, 4Q505, 4Q507–509, p. 28) contain formal elements that suggest a common origin in temple liturgy. In contrast, 4QDaily Prayers (4Q503–504), fragmentarily preserved, seems to be a text written within the Union.

Before the turn of the era, prescribed prayer and liturgy were primarily celebrated in the temple, led by priests and Levites. In the Qumran movement there is a "democratization" of prayer—each member of the community performs his daily prayers, if possible, gathered in a group.

Since the Union withdrew from the Hasmonean temple due to disagreements about purity and the festival calendar, they held the service of the Jerusalem temple to be far from God's primary will. This led the Union to regard itself as a spiritual temple, "a temple of men," where their prayers and liturgies substituted for temple sacrifices. A similar rethinking would appear in the New Testament (John 2:19–21; Eph 2:20–22; 1 Pet 2:4–10), and subsequently in the rabbinic movement after the catastrophic defeat of the Bar Kokhba revolt (132–136 CE), when Israel lost their hopes of rebuilding the temple in the foreseeable future.

For Further Reading

Falk, Daniel K. "Festival Prayers." In *Outside the Bible: Ancient Jewish Writings Related in Scripture*, edited by Louis H. Feldman et al., 1939–59. 3 vols. Philadelphia: Jewish Publication Society, 2013.

Words of the Luminaries

pp. 30–32.

Words of the (heavenly) Luminaries is preserved in two scrolls, 4Q504 and 4Q506. Since the fragments from the scrolls overlap, a substantial part of these texts can be restored.

Words of the Luminaries is a daily liturgy that the Qumran movement likely had inherited from temple circles. It does not bear the characteristics of the Union; the prayers reflect a common Judean piety of pre-Maccabean times.

Daniel Falk notes the contrast between these prayers and biblical psalms, where there were no set times for communal or individual prayers, and people prayed when they felt they needed to or wanted to. "Luminaries is the earliest example of a new attitude toward prayer that became the hallmark of the synagogue: prayer as a religious service to God. Together the community confesses sin and prays for spiritual and physical help at regular times, bringing all of life before God and expressing complete dependence on God." Falk further notes parallels between Luminaries and the Amidah, the daily prayer formulated after the fall of the temple: both raise before God desires for knowledge, forgiveness, redemption, healing, and restoration of Jerusalem and the Davidic dynasty, in both there is a contrast between the righteous and the wicked (Falk, "Words of the Luminaries," 1960–61). If Luminaries is indeed pre-Qumranic, it was not a common liturgy for Israelites at large but would have been used in more limited circles, perhaps by the Levites of the temple.

This liturgy was probably recited at sunrise and sunset and repeated each week of the year. The Sabbath prayer is a hymn of praise, while the prayers for the other weekdays are petitions for God to forgive, to help the people keep God's torah, and to rescue them from physical or spiritual distress.

Falk, Daniel K. "Daily Prayers." In *Outside the Bible: Ancient Jewish Writings Related in Scripture*, edited by Louis H. Feldman et al., 1927–38. 3 vols. Philadelphia: Jewish Publication Society, 2013.

———. "Words of the Luminaries." In *Outside the Bible: Ancient Jewish Writings Related in Scripture*, edited by Louis H. Feldman et al., 1960–84. 3 vols. Philadelphia: Jewish Publication Society, 2013.

Newman, Judith H. "Words of the Luminaries." In *T&T Clark Companion to the Dead Sea Scrolls*, edited by George J. Brooke and Charlotte Hempel, 365–66. T. & T. Clark Companions. London: T. & T. Clark, 2019.

Psalms of Solomon

pp. 33–36, 55–56, 59–62, 65, 116–19.

Some of the church fathers had knowledge of eighteen Psalms of Solomon. Only in the seventeenth century, however, were these psalms identified in a Greek manuscript and subsequently published. The psalms were written in Hebrew language in the period 90–40 BCE. Some of them polemize against the leading priestly circles in Jerusalem, seen as too liberal and deviating from the right path. The psalms reveal a more optimistic anthropology than the Thanksgiving Hymns; the view of man here can be compared with the book of Sirach. An earlier generation of scholars associated these psalms with the Pharisees, a connection less stressed today. If Ps Sol 11, hailing the influx of Jewish immigrants to the land, should be dated to around 100 BCE (pp. 55–56), the same authorial circle is not necessarily behind all the psalms.

These psalms echo and allude to prophetic and poetic biblical texts. In Ps Sol 7 we sense that the national independence and integrity of Judea is under threat. The land and the temple are in danger of being trampled down by an enemy nation, a reference to the rising power of Rome with its armies. The psalm petitions God to show mercy toward the nation he has elected, and the temple, the dwelling place of his presence. On behalf of their nation these singers pray that God will come near and save them from their threatening enemy.

The psalms are preserved in Greek and Syriac. Most scholars argue that they were written in Hebrew, while a Judean author writing in Greek heavily influenced by the Septuagint has also been suggested. The Psalms of Solomon were not found in Qumran—the traditionalist Essenes held to a narrower ecclesiology; for them salvation belonged to their own community only. The last two psalms express a hope for the Davidic messiah. Here Pompey's removal of the Hasmonean rulers is seen as a well-deserved judgment on a leadership that had failed and not heeded God's guidance (see pp. 116–19).

The Book of Judith

pp. 37–38.

Like its older relative Tobit, the novel Judith is set in early Israelite history: the Babylonian king Nebuchadnezzar (here called "king of the Assyrians") and his commander Holofernes are making war against Judah and besiege a Judean city called Bethulia, a city guarding the way to Jerusalem. When Judahite men are powerless, the beautiful and godfearing widow Judith appears as the one who can save the nation. In the middle of the enemy's war camp, she charms Holofernes and gets him drunk, beheads the general, and brings his head as a trophy back to her city, without having been defiled by extramarital sex.

The book employs irony, double meanings, humor, sexual tension, and suspense. It raises questions about leadership and gender roles. It contrasts pagan and Judean, war and beauty, a powerful army and a solitary woman, thirst inside the besieged city and Holofernes's excessive drinking. God remains in the background while Judith takes the initiative. She continues the line of female heroes and tricksters in the Bible: Rebekah (Gen 27–28), Tamar (Gen 38), the midwives, Moses's mother and sister (Exod 1–2), Rahab (Josh 2; 6), Deborah (Judg 4–5), and Jael (Judg 4). Judith appears as the ideal woman: beautiful, loyal, pious, and ascetic. She symbolizes the way through repentance to salvation, for the individual and the nation.

Judith was written in the late second or early first century BCE; it shows dependence on Daniel as well as on 1 and 2 Maccabees. The book's hailing of a female hero has led some recent interpreters to suggest that it is a symbolic laudation of Queen Salome Alexandra, who ruled the Judean state for nine years after the death of her husband Alexander Jannaeus in 76 BCE. Like the fictional Judith, Salome enjoyed popularity in her nation.

For Further Reading

Gera, Deborah Levine. *Judith*. Commentaries on Early Jewish Literature. Berlin: de Gruyter, 2014.

Wills, Lawrence M. *Judith: A Commentary on the Book of Judith*. Hermeneia. Minneapolis: Fortress, 2019.

2 Maccabees

pp. 39–42.

Second Maccabees is contained only in one of the three large Greek Bibles from ca. 400 CE, Codex Alexandrinus, but the Greek text appears in many other manuscripts.

Second Maccabees is no continuation of 1 Maccabees (on 1 Maccabees, see pp. 202–4). It introduces itself as a condensed version of a long historical narrative written by Jason of Cyrene (in Libya), a writer not known from other sources—the reference to Jason may be a literary foil intended to enhance the trustworthiness of the book. The story starts under the high priesthood of Onias III and narrates civil strife in Jerusalem and Seleucid aggression against Jerusalem and the temple, culminating under Antiochus Epiphanes. Antiochus makes Jerusalem a Hellenistic city, has a gymnasium built, and proscribes obedience to the ancestral laws. Some Judeans choose martyrdom rather than submitting to the ungodly king, while the Maccabean brothers turn to guerilla warfare against the Syrians (as 2 Maccabees designates the Seleucids). Subsequently, the God of Israel humbles Antiochus through an accident and sickness that leads to his death. The Maccabees lead the cleansing and rededication of the temple. Fighting with the Syrian armies continues, and the book ends with Judah the Maccabee leading a celebration of victory in Jerusalem after the death of the enemy commander Nicanor, calling for the institution of "Nicanor's Day" as an annual Judean festival.

Compared with 1 Maccabees, the book has a more legendary character. The number of those who fall in battles is exaggerated, and the book records many divine interventions that contribute to the victories of the Judeans and the humiliation of their enemies. The historical storyline is shorter than that of 1 Maccabees: it begins with the high priesthood of Onias III around 175 BCE and ends before the death of Judah the Maccabee in 160.

Important theological themes in the book are martyrdom, the afterlife of the soul, and the hope for bodily resurrection. Another central motif is the Lord's zeal for his temple. Jews are admonished to be faithful to their ancestral traditions and to keep some distance from Hellenistic culture. At the same time, the author insists that Jews can live in peace with local gentile communities and with an imperial power.[2]

As a prelude to the narrative, a later editor added two letters from the community in Jerusalem to Jews in Egypt about the celebration of Hanukkah (1:1–10a; 1:10b—2:18). The first letter, likely written in 124 BCE, calls the festival "the days of building booths in the month of Kislev," a designation recurring in the second letter (1:9, 18). The second letter to Jews in Egypt purports to be written by Judah the Maccabee and the elders of Jerusalem in the 160s BCE. This is likely a rhetorical device by a scribe writing sometime in the

2. Doran, *2 Maccabees*, 13–14.

late second century BCE: the letter reflects the conditions in a stable Hasmonean state that seeks to enlarge its population. The first translation from 2 Maccabees—Nehemiah's temple prayer at the Festival of Booths—is part of the Nehemiah legend contained in the second letter.

According to the second letter, Judah the Maccabee founded a library that contained the Scriptures from the past. This passage (2:13–15) may suggest the presence of a royal library in Jerusalem from the time of John Hyrcanus (134–105 BCE), a library with literature in Hebrew, Aramaic, and Greek. For example, some of the first-century-BCE authors of the Song of Songs were acquainted with the poems of the Greek writer Theocritus.

When the book received its additions, the celebration of Hanukkah was already well established in Judea. Further, the main narrative refers to "the day of Mordechai," later called Purim, in the winter month of Adar, immediately following the celebration of the triumph on the "Day of Nicanor" in 161 BCE (2 Macc 15:36—the earliest reference to Purim outside the book of Esther). Verses 1–8 of chapter 10 report the cleansing of the temple and the institution of festival days in the month of Kislev.

The early name Hanukkah, "the days of building booths," is explained in 2 Macc 10: hiding in the Judean highlands, the Maccabean guerilla fighters could not celebrate the Festival of Booths in the temple at its set time. When they later liberated Jerusalem and the temple, they could celebrate an eight-day "festival of booths" after a two-month delay, which in its turn became the origin of "the festival of the dedication of the altar" (1 Macc 4:59).

> They celebrated eight days of rejoicing, in the manner of Booths, remembering how not long before, during the Festival of Booths, they had been living in the mountains and caverns like wild animals. Therefore, carrying wreaths, leafy boughs and branches of palms, they offered hymns to him who had given success to the purifying of his holy place. They decreed by public edict and by vote that the whole nation of the Judeans should celebrate these days every year. (2 Macc 10:6–8)

Scholars commonly date the main narrative to the generations around 100 BCE and suggest a Jewish author writing in Greek either in Jerusalem or somewhere in the diaspora (in Alexandria or Asia Minor). Chapter 4 provides information on a revolt against Antiochus in Asia Minor, a revolt that is not known from other sources, and 8:20 reports an otherwise unknown battle against Galatians—features that might suggest Asia Minor as the place of origin: Robert Doran suggests this in a personal communication, while Daniel Schwartz looks more toward Alexandria. In contrast, John Ma argues that the four letters included in 2 Macc 11:16–38 had been preserved in the archive of the temple, which would make a Judean provenance a more likely option.

Second Maccabees argues strongly against Jews going to gymnasia for sport—a cultural challenge for Jews from the late second century onwards. Inscriptions referring to Jews going to gymnasia around the Greek world appear after 105 BCE. In 5:23 and 6:2 we sense a positive appraisal of Mount Gerizim as belonging to the Judean nation, and no enmity towards the Samaritans. This may place the composition of the main narrative before John Hyrcanus's violent destruction of Garizim and the Samaritan city of Shechem in 111 BCE. I would tentatively place the narrative in Judea between 120 and 111, a decade or two after the composition of 1 Maccabees; furthermore, I would date to the early first century BCE the editorial additions of the two letters at the start of 2 Maccabees.

During the last decade, John Ma and Sylvi Honigman have suggested that the liberation and rededication of the temple that led to Hanukkah in December 164 BCE was implemented not by Judah the Maccabee but by the high priest Menelaos. In their reading of the letters included in 2 Macc 11:16–38, they note that 11:27–33 (a letter from Antiochus V to the Judean nation after the death of Antiochus Epiphanes) refers to Menelaos as the mediator between the nation and the new Seleucid boy-king, who decided to cancel his father's punitive measures against the Judeans. For Ma and Honigman, 1 and 2 Maccabees have recast Judah the Maccabee and the Hasmonean family as the heroes of 164 BCE and the originators of Hanukka—as Judah indeed was the hero of the battle against Nicanor and of the institution of Nicanor's Day in 161 BCE; by then Menelaus had already been executed by the Seleucids.

In both 1 and 2 Maccabees, Hanukkah and Nicanor's Day become mnemonic events that legitimize the Hasmonean dynasty in the collective memory, and that memorialize victories against enemies that threatened the Judean nation and its temple (1 Macc 4 and 7; 2 Macc 10 and 15).

Archaeological finds may bolster Ma and Honigman's hypothesis about Menelaos as the true hero of the rededication of the temple. The notion of widespread upheaval in the days of Judah the Maccabee, as described in 1 and 2 Maccabees, is not heavily supported by archaeological evidence. Few destruction layers from the 160s have been identified. In contrast, from the time of the intra-Seleucid wars in the 140s, a number of destruction layers have been found around in Judea at large.

Thus, the authors of 1 and 2 Maccabees may have created a narrative doublet based on the troubles of the mid-140s, which are archaeologically well documented. These two pro-Hasmonean authors could have redated to the days of Antiochus IV victories that were actually achieved at a later time, when the Maccabees took advantage of the Seleucid dynastic quarrels to rise to power. Indeed, the substantial expansion of Hasmonean-controlled territory began around 140 BCE. The map in figure 4 (p. 107) shows the exponential growth of Hasmonean territory from the time of Simon (142–134) onwards.

For Further Reading

Berlin, Andrea M., and Paul J. Kosmin, eds. *The Middle Maccabees: Archaeology, History, and the Rise of the Hasmonean Kingdom*. Archaeology and Biblical Studies 28. Atlanta: SBL Press, 2021.

Doran, Robert. 2 *Maccabees: A Critical Commentary.* Hermeneia. Minneapolis: Fortress, 2012.

Honigman, Sylvie. *Tales of High Priests and Taxes: The Books of the Maccabees and the Judean Rebellion against Antiochus IV.* Hellenistic Culture and Society 56. Berkeley: University of California Press, 2014.

Ma, John. "Re-Examining Hanukkah." *Marginalia Review of Books*, July 9, 2013. https://themarginaliareview.com/re-examining-hanukkah/.

Rhyder, Julia. "Hellenizing Hanukkah: The Commemoration of Military Victory in the Books of the Maccabees." In *Collective Violence and Memory in the Ancient Mediterranean*, edited by Sonja Ammann et al., 92–109. Culture and History of the Ancient Near East 135. Leiden: Brill, 2023,

Sirach

pp. 47–48, 66–67, 79–80, 98

From a theological viewpoint, the book of Sirach may be considered the most important of the Old Testament Apocrypha. Around 190, Yeshua ben Sira led a school in Jerusalem for the sons of Jerusalem's small elite (51:23).

His book was written in Hebrew and subsequently translated into Greek. The Greek translator opens the book with a long introduction: as Ben Sira's grandson, he made a Greek translation of this book in Egypt "in the thirty-eighth year of king Euergetes" (=130 BCE). This "origin story" may in fact be the invention of a later scribe who made his translation around the start of the first century CE.

Only the Greek version is completely preserved, as part of the Old Testament Apocrypha. Small fragments of a Hebrew copy were found in Qumran, and of another at Masada. Five more substantial, but also fragmentary copies from medieval times were recovered from the Cairo Genizah, the archival room of the Cairo Karaite synagogue in the late nineteenth century. Both the Greek and the Hebrew texts were subject to editing during the early centuries—often it is difficult to restore the author's original text.

Sirach is an instructional wisdom book, in part reminiscent of Proverbs. The author draws on his experience in teaching elite young men in Jerusalem; most of his book likely belonged to the curriculum. Ben Sira is closely related to the temple establishment. He includes a glorious description of the present high priest, Simon II (218–192) celebrating the liturgy (50:5–21), and portrays Simon acting as civil leader of the people (50:1–4). Simon is praised for renovating the temple precincts after the Seleucids conquered Jerusalem in 198 BCE and gave prerogatives to the temple city. During the 1970s, the Israeli archaeologist Yoram Tsafrir indeed identified pre-Hasmonean restoration of the Eastern wall of the Temple Mount, with Hasmonean layers on top.

The prayer on p. 47 is part of the last psalm in a sequence of poems, perhaps composed by Ben Sira himself (34:21–31; 35:1–13, 14–22a, 22b–26; 36:1–22). In theme and form, 36:1–22 contrasts with the preceding poems that are permeated by wisdom instruction. Thus, Ben Sira may here have inserted an earlier psalm.

In Ben Sira's time, the high priest was the religious and civil leader of the Judeans and their province, a situation that may have influenced his eschatology. His main hope is an ingathering of the exiles and a glorious restoration of Zion and the temple, without any mention of a Davidic ruler.

For Further Reading

Adams, Samuel et al., eds. *Sirach and Its Contexts: The Pursuit of Wisdom and Human Flourishing*. Journal for the Study of Judaism Supplements 196. Leiden: Brill, 2021.

Askin, Lindsey A. *Scribal Culture in Ben Sira*. Journal for the Study of Judaism Supplements 184. Leiden: Brill, 2018.

Tobit

pp. 49–52.

The book of Tobit is part of the Old Testament Apocrypha or the deuterocanonical books. It is a short story written in Aramaic, probably between 225 and 175 BCE. The author may be located either in Judea or in the Eastern diaspora. Fitzmyer tends toward Judea, since the author is not well informed about the geography in the East. In the penultimate chapter, two hymns were editorially included into the narrative (13:1–8, 9–18): the latter, which focuses on the restoration of Zion, is included here.

Tobit is a folkloristic short story set among Israelites exiled to Assyria after the fall of the Northern Kingdom. The main actors are Tobit and his son Tobias, living in Nineveh, and far away in Media their young relative Sarah, who is plagued by an evil spirit. Tobit becomes blind, and subsequently sends Tobias on a business journey to Media. A stranger appears and accompanies Tobias on his journey—this is God's angel Raphael in disguise. While they are on their way, Raphael reveals to Tobias how he can heal his father's blindness and cure his relative Sarah, the maiden destined to be his bride. Tobias ends up marrying Sarah, and on his return home he heals his father. The story ends with Tobit giving his son admonitions on a righteous life and lifting his voice in praise to God, concluding "Let all men speak about his greatness, his praises be sung in Jerusalem" (13:8, the end of a hymn added by an early editor). Tobit's hymn of praise thus closes with blessings to be sung in Jerusalem, and a second editor found it pertinent to include the Zion hymn rendered here.

Tobit can be read as an allegory. Tobit and Sarah symbolize Israel's plight and suffering—exile and life in the diaspora. Their healing signals hope and mercy for the people. According to both psalms included in Tobit 13, God will afflict Israel for their evil deeds but will again show them mercy by gathering them from the nations to their native land, where Jerusalem and the temple will see a glorious future. In Christian tradition, Tobit enjoys popularity also as a marriage story.

Tobit exists in two main recensions: a longer one preserved in Sinaiticus (followed here) and a shorter one, represented by Alexandrinus and Vaticanus. A third, hybrid version, mixes the two main recensions. A comparison of these versions with the five Qumran manuscripts (four in Aramaic, one in Hebrew) suggests that the longer recension is the more original. Parts of the hymns included in Tobit 13 are preserved in two Qumran manuscripts, one dated to ca. 50 BCE, the other to the turn of the era, which means that both hymns were added relatively early, probably sometime in the second century BCE.

The hymn rendered here was likely composed in Hebrew, not the Aramaic of Tobit's story. Centuries later, the Spanish poet Judah Halevi (ca. 1075–1141) would cultivate and refine the "ode to Zion" literary form. One of his odes to Zion would, in turn, be an inspiration for Naomi Shemer's song "Jerusalem of Gold." She would turn around Judah's words to Zion: "Dreaming of the end of your exile, I will be a harp for your songs (*ani kinor ləshirayik*)."

In the translation from Tob 13, as in the translation from Sir 36, the hope for the end-time focuses on a restoration of Zion without any mention of a son of David. In only two stanzas is attention given to the temple: "that your temple may be rebuilt with joy within you"; and, "Jerusalem shall be built anew, his house for ever and ever." The hymn focuses on the glorious redemption of Jerusalem, which will include the nations making pilgrimages to Zion, as in Isa 5.

For Further Reading

Fitzmyer, Joseph A. *Tobit.* Commentaries on Early Jewish Literature. Berlin: de Gruyter, 2003.

Psalms of Solomon 11

pp. 55–56.

Inspired by texts from Isa 34–35 and 40–55, Ps Sol 11 illustrates the return of the dispersed Judeans and the resettling of the people, seen from the perspective of Jerusalem. This is no prophecy about an unspecified future, but a description of the influx of Judean immigrants to the steadily growing Hasmonean state in the late second and early first centuries. One could also point to the inclusion of the Idumeans in the Judean "commonwealth" in 107 BCE, which enlarged the state and added to its population and power.

The migration is seen as fulfillment of Isaianic oracles (particularly 40:3–4, 9–11; 49:11–12; 52:7–9; 60:4), though no messiah is mentioned. Full redemption may not yet have arrived, but one senses the outpouring of end-time blessings. Different from other psalms in the collection (such as 17:4–9, 20, see p. 116), this hymn does not signal any criticism of the Hasmonean rulers and their military enterprise, and we may be close to the pro-Hasmonean ideology of 1 Maccabees and the blessing of a Hasmonean king (pp. 112–14).

For Further Reading

Elgvin, Torleif. *Warrior, King, Servant, Savior: Messianism in the Hebrew Bible and Early Jewish Texts*, 226–27. Grand Rapids: Eerdmans, 2022.

Early Jewish Beatitudes

pp. 63–64.

The genre of the beatitude belongs to the biblical wisdom books. It is known from the books of Psalms, Proverbs, Sirach, and 1 Enoch, and from the preaching of Jesus: those fearing God are declared righteous and are promised reward, either in this life or in the hereafter. In the Hebrew Bible and Sirach, the beatitudes have this life as horizon—God rewards the pious with happiness and a good life. The same goes for the Psalms of Solomon (see Ps Sol 6, p. 65). In 1 Enoch and Jesus' Sermon on the Mount, one senses an end-time perspective: the day of judgment is close at hand and the time of redemption is near. To the true disciples God will speak comfort and a presence that outlasts death.

The perspective of the beatitudes of 4Q525 is life on this side, with Ps 1 as a main text of reference. The pious listens to the instruction of his teacher and follows the rules of God. There are formal parallels here with the beatitudes of Jesus in Matt 5. The Qumran text contains four short beatitudes followed by a longer one, while Matthew presents 4 + 4 short ones followed by one longer one. Thus, 4 + 1 beatitudes may have been a common form among Judean wisdom teachers.

The "catechism" of 4Q525 does not bear the color of the Qumran movement; it represents common Judean piety. The text speaks about the Wisdom from God. As in Prov 1–9, so also here Lady Wisdom is God's mouth and messenger—God relates to humans through his Wisdom. 4Q525 parallels Wisdom with God's torah, "the guidance of the Most High." The torah is, however, not identified with the books of Moses.

In some texts, Matthew depicts Jesus as a Judean wisdom teacher. According to Matt 11:19, 28–30, Jesus introduces himself as Wisdom who speaks on God's behalf. The idea that Jesus embodies God's Wisdom (as portrayed in Prov 1–9 and Sir 1; 6; 24) would be essential when the early church reflected about Christ's nature as it related to the Father. Texts such as John 1:1–14; Col 1:15–20; Heb 1:3, and the later Nicene Creed would identify Christ with preexisting Wisdom.

For Further Reading

Peters, Dorothy M. "Beatitudes." In *T. & T. Clark Companion to the Dead Sea Scrolls*, edited by George J. Brooke and Charlotte Hempel, 295–97. T. & T. Clark Companions. London: T. & T. Clark, 2019.

Joseph and Aseneth

pp. 71–75.

Joseph and Aseneth is among the many writings elaborating passages from the Hebrew Bible. Short notes in the Bible would inspire the fantasy of later interpreters, who tried to "read between the lines" in biblical stories. Joseph and Aseneth was written in Greek, the language of the Jews of Egypt. Being the daughter of a high priest in the temple city of On (Heliopolis), Aseneth was bound to worship the Egyptian gods. Marrying Joseph, she gave birth to Ephraim and Manasseh—the ancestors of two of the main tribes of Israel. Jewish interpreters would ask how Joseph, the pious Israelite, could marry the daughter of a priest, who worshiped idols. So, stories about Aseneth were written; in most of them she ultimately confesses the faith of Israel.

Joseph and Aseneth is a long novel about human love and the presence of the God of Israel in the land of Egypt. Romanticism, apologetics for Israel's faith, and confidence in God's dwelling among Judeans in Egypt are interweaved. The proud young Aseneth is struck by awe in her encounter with Joseph and his God. She recognizes the illusion that the idols represent, makes penitence, and prostrates herself before the God of Israel. Her long, emotional prayer is rendered here—a touching petition to a Father in heaven, full of love and empathy. After this prayer, an angel of God descends to Aseneth. He proclaims that she has found mercy with God and blesses her forthcoming marriage to Joseph. The book continues as an exciting crime novel. Pharaoh's son desires the beautiful Aseneth and conspires with some of Joseph's brothers to kidnap her. Finally, she is rescued by Joseph's brother Levi and some of his peers.

Different scholars have suggested dating the book sometime between the second century BCE and the fourth century CE. Some of them propose a Jewish author and a later Christian polisher. Phrases in the book have parallels in the Gospel of John and other early Christian writings; the main motif of Aseneth's prayer can be compared with Jesus' parable of the prodigal son and the loving father. Further, the angel proclaims that Aseneth will be a role model for "many nations" who will receive the true faith. So for both Jews and Christians the book could have functioned as a refutation of polytheism in the face of the many gods of the nations. Joseph and Aseneth was known among Christians from the late fourth century and became popular in many churches. Its image of God as a caring father was dear both to Jews and Christians.

I tend to follow the hypothesis of Gideon Bohak (1996), who argues that Joseph and Aseneth was written as a defense of the Jewish community that in the 160s BCE founded a temple of the Lord in Heliopolis. In 175 the high priest Onias III was ousted from his office in the Jerusalem temple. He was later killed in Antioch (2 Macc 4), and his son Onias IV led a group of Judeans into Egypt where he received Pharaoh's permission to build a sanctuary for the Lord in the temple city of Heliopolis. Soon this community would find support in the Greek translation of Isaiah (probably made in Alexandria by the mid-second century), and several verses from it could easily have been read as prophecies about the new temple and its high priest Onias, the man who would lead this exiled community:

> On that day there will be five cities in Egypt speaking the language of Canaan and swearing in the name of the Lord, and one city will be called the City of Righteousness or the City of the Sun (=Heliopolis). On that day there will be an altar to the Lord in the land of the Egyptians and a memorial stele to the Lord at its border . . . When they cry to the Lord because of oppressors, the Lord will send them a man who will save them. (19:18–20)
>
> The Lord will bring up against you the strong waters of the Great River, the king of the Assyrians (=Antiochus Epiphanes) and his glory . . . and He will take away from Judea a man who can lift his head and accomplish great things; his camp will fill the breadth of your country—God is with us. (8:7–8)
>
> O, my people who live in Zion, do not be afraid of the Assyrians when they strike you with a rod, for I will strike you so that you will see the way of Egypt. (10:24)

In chapters 16–17, of Joseph and Aseneth, Aseneth is shown a honeycomb with the scent of paradise. Then a swarm of bees rises from the comb and makes a new one on her lips. The first comb is subsequently devoured by fire, so that only the new one remains. The first comb is a symbol of the Jerusalem temple, now without God's presence and destined for destruction, while the second points to the new temple of Heliopolis.

Aseneth is told that she has eaten the bread of life and drunk the cup of immortality; she will be like a walled mother-city to all who seek refuge in the name of the Lord. The sons of the Living God will dwell in her city of refuge. Those who are chosen will be called from darkness to light, from death to life; they will be renewed by God's spirit and enjoy God's eternal life forever and ever (16:14; 19:9; 8:10–11).

For Gideon Bohak, the book represents a moderate messianism. The story may be read as an allegory of the two temples and the exile of Onias: the anointed high priest and his community will establish a city that will be the end-time Jerusalem; their temple will be God's dwelling and a source of life for Judeans as well as Egyptian converts who follow the path of Aseneth.

For Further Reading

Bohak, Gideon. *Joseph and Aseneth and the Jewish Temple in Heliopolis*. Early Judaism and Its Literature 10. Atlanta: Scholars, 1996.

Elgvin, Torleif. *Warrior, King, Servant, Savior*, 191–97.

Prayer of Manasseh

pp. 76–78.

Bruce Metzger called the Prayer of Manasseh "one of the finest pieces in the Apocrypha," a typical example of Jewish penitential prayer.[3] It was written possibly during the last two centuries BCE, and most probably penned in Greek. It is included in one of the early Septuagint codices, Codex Alexandrinus, and in some medieval Vulgate manuscripts. In some Greek manuscripts it appears as a liturgical appendix to the book of Psalms. A Syriac translation appears in the early *Didascalia apostolorum* (around 230 CE). A medieval Hebrew version was found in the Cairo Genizah, the archival room of the ancient Karaite synagogue—this "rabbinic version" probably goes back to a translation from Syriac. The Roman Catholic Church does not count the Prayer of Manasseh as a deuterocanonical writing, while Protestant churches include it within the Old Testament Apocrypha.

For further reading

Metzger, Bruce M. *An Introduction to the Apocrypha*, 123–28. New York: Oxford University Press, 1957. Reprint, 1963.

Sensuality from Ben Sira to the Song of Songs

pp. 79–80.

Ben Sira's sensual description of his longing for Wisdom from above inspired Jewish writers in generations to follow. The Genesis Apocryphon from Cave 1 is a colorful second-century retelling in Aramaic of chapters from Genesis, concentrating on the stories about Enoch, Noah, and Abraham. In the retelling of Gen 20, the envoys of King Abimelech tell their master that Sarah, the "sister" of the wise Hebrew immigrant, could be an attractive member of his harem.

> How beautiful her face is; how gorgeous is her hair. Her eyes are lovely, her nose pleasant, and her face is radiant [. . .] How shapely are her breasts, how gorgeous all her fairness. Her arms are comely and her hands perfect. Her

3. Metzger, *Introduction to the Apocrypha*, 123–28.

> palms are exquisite, her fingers long and delicate. Her thighs are perfect and "her feet" attractive. Neither virgins nor brides entering the bridal chamber exceed her charms. Over all women is her beauty supreme, her loveliness far above them all. Yet with all this comeliness, she possesses great wisdom. Yea, all that she has is beautiful. (1QapGen 20:3–8)

By the mid-first century BCE, the Wisdom of Solomon would follow suit.

> Wisdom reaches mightily from one end of the earth to the other . . . I fell in love with her beauty; I sought her from my youth. / I desired to take her for my bride / and became enamored of her beauty. (8:1–2)

In time, Ben Sira's sensual song would inspire some of the first-century poets who gave us the Song of Songs, poets who praised sensual love—both as experienced between a man and a woman, and as a reflection of God's love for his people. In the lacunae of the last two lines of his poem, I have tentatively restored phrases that later recur in Song 3:6. Based on the Qumran scrolls of the Song of Songs I argued in a 2018 monograph that Canticles was written after Sirach.[4]

For Further Reading

Elgvin, Torleif. "The Song of Songs: Torah, Creation, Celebration, and Libertinism." In *Between Wisdom and Torah: Discourses on Wisdom and Law in Second Temple Judaism*, edited by Jiseong J. Kwon and Seth A. Bledsoe, 243–74. Deuterocanonical and Cognate Literature Studies 51. Berlin: de Gruyter, 2023.

4. Elgvin, *The Literary Growth of the Song of Songs.*

Essene and New Testament Anthropology

pp. 12–13, 87–97.

In Paul's Letters we encounter an anthropology similar to that of the Essenes. Both the apostle and the Essenes could confess that God in his mercy justifies the ungodly, a theme later stressed by Saint Augustine and Martin Luther.

If a Pharisee had discussed with an Essene the interpretation of Ps 51, the Pharisee would possibly have responded as follows: With the words "I was born guilty, a sinner when my mother conceived me," David was talking about himself, not about the sons of men in general. Reading Ps 51:5 together with 1 Sam 16, one might deduce that David could have been born out of wedlock: he looked different from his seven brothers, and Jesse had left David out on purpose when Samuel the prophet had asked Jesse to bring his sons before hm; a variation of this explanatory story appears in the late midrash Yalkut HaMachiri.

Other themes recurring in New Testament Letters are not difficult to find in the Qumranite corpus: God's wisdom cannot be scrutinized by men (Rom 11:33–36); his wisdom and plan of salvation are hidden for men in general but revealed to his elect community (1 Cor 1:17–25; Eph 1:8–14); the community is a spiritual temple enjoying communion with the angels above (1 Pet 2:5; Rev 4–5).

Ps 151A

pp. 103–4.

The book of Psalms, regularly inscribed on two scrolls, grew into its final form throughout the second century BCE. The first scroll would commonly conclude with the messianic Ps 72; the second scroll ended alternatively with Ps 150 or 151. The version with 151 psalms was translated into Greek in Alexandria early in the first century BCE. This version is followed in some later Syriac Bibles—reflecting the view that the Psalter should end with an expressed Davidic hope.

Ps 151 is preserved toward the end of the large Psalms Scroll, 11QPs[a], which demonstrates that the Greek Ps 151 is a conflation of two psalms where David sings about his odyssey and career. The first of these two psalms is rendered here in its more elaborate and complete Hebrew version. The second psalm sings about David's fight with Goliath. 11QPs[a] preserves the beginning of this second psalm, while the Greek text jumps directly from "the Lord did not choose them" in Ps 151A to the end of Ps 151B (Ps 151:6–7).

11QPs[a] ends with David's last words, from 2 Sam 21:1–7; these are followed by a resume-like list of all the songs of David and then by Pss 140, 134:1–3, and Pss 151A and 151B: due to the deterioration of the scroll, the end of 151B was not preserved. Thus, this "hymnbook" of the Qumranite Union was consciously formatted with a Davidic-messianic ending.

For Further Reading

Elgvin, Torleif. *Warrior, King, Servant, Savior*, 167–72.

1 Maccabees

pp. 105–11.

After more than four hundred years of subjugation under world empires, the Maccabean brothers led the Judean nation to enjoy independence under their own leaders. Under this Hasmonean family Judea was transformed from a small province around the temple to a large and powerful state, extending the borders of the Israelite state further than any time in Israelite history. Figures 3 and 4 (pp. 107–8) illustrate the exponential growth of Judea and Jerusalem between 160 and 80 BCE.

1 Maccabees was written by a Hasmonean court historian around the 120s BCE, likely commissioned by John Hyrcanus, Hasmonean ruler, and high priest. The book was soon translated into Greek, serving as a pro-Hasmonean piece of propaganda.

The Hebrew original is not preserved. As many early Jewish texts, 1 and 2 Maccabees were transmitted and preserved in church circles, faithfully copied for generations in the monasteries of the Middle East. Up to the time of the Reformation, most Christian Bibles contained 1 and 2 Maccabees.

1 Maccabees records the persecution of the Jews by the Seleucid king Antiochus IV Epiphanes in the early 160s, the subsequent Maccabean revolt, the cleansing of the temple in 164, and the continued fights and rule of the Maccabean (Hasmonean) brothers, Judah the Maccabee, Jonathan, and Simon, as well as the early years of Simon's son, John Hyrcanus.

The author, likely connected to a royal-sponsored library in Jerusalem, is well versed in the Scriptures and often alludes to biblical verses. At times he uses fictional historical stories and humor to convey a partly hidden message. For him, Hasmonean history is part of biblical history. The Hasmoneans are divinely sent redeemers of the Judean nation because of their faithfulness to the ancestral teaching of the Judeans. The style of the book can be compared to the books of Samuel, Kings, and Chronicles. In contrast to these, the author usually does not attribute victory to divine intervention. Military victories and the rapid growth of the state derive from the strength and wisdom of the Maccabean brothers.

In chapters 3 and 14, the historical storyline is supplemented by two laudatory poems on Judah the Maccabee (died 160) and his brother Simon (died 134). With their poetic form and many allusions to biblical passages these songs stand out from other texts in 1 Maccabees. The poems demonstrate that many viewed the Hasmonean rulers as precursors of the messianic age, in fact fulfilling many messianic promises on the ground. One could paint these priestly rulers in messianic colors even though the full realization of the promises still would be in the future—a combination of a present and a future messianism—a feature that later can be observed in the gospels of the New Testament.

This laudation of the leader of the revolt, Judah the Maccabee, could have been written soon after his death in battle 160 BCE, or later as a pendent to the laudation of Simon, composed soon after the death of the latter. When Judah "brought bitterness to many kings," the eulogy would allude to royal psalms such as Ps 2:1–4, 10–12 and 110:1–2, 5–6.

For Further Reading

Atkinson, Kenneth. *A History of the Hasmonean State: Josephus and Beyond.* London: Bloomsbury, 2016.

Elgvin, Torleif. *Warrior, King, Servant, Savior*, 210–20.

Eshel, Hanan. *The Dead Sea Scrolls and the Hasmonean State.* Grand Rapids and Jerusalem: Eerdmans and Yad Ben-Zvi, 2008.

Simon the Hasmonean

pp. 109–11.

The laudation of Simon could have been written soon after his death and would also serve as legitimation of his son John Hyrcanus as ruler of the nation. The poem draws on messianic texts such as Ps 2:9; 72:8; 110:2, 5, 6; Isa 11:4; Mic 4:4; 5:4–5. The "Citadel" refers to the Acra fortress, built on a high place close to the temple by the Syrian king Antiochus Epiphanes soon after 170 (the foundations of the Acra have recently been identified in the Givati excavations outside the Dung Gate). The fortress remained in the hand of the Syrians until the reign of Simon.

When Simon made Joppa (=Jaffa) "an entranceway to the islands of the sea and extended the borders of his nation," he fulfilled prophecies of the future Davidic rule reaching "from the sea to the sea" and "from the Great River to the sea," (Ps 72:8; Zech 9:10; Ps 89:25). "They farmed their land in peace," "each man sat under his own vine and fig tree," and "he established peace in the land" allude to Mic 4:4 and 5:3–4. "No enemy was left in the land to fight them, and the kings were crushed in those days" echoes Ps 2:9 and 110:2,

5. "His fame resounded to the end of the earth" recalls Ps 72:8. And "he gave help to all the needy among his people" points to the messianic promise in Isa 11:4. When Simon "gavenew splendor to the temple, replenishing it with sacred vessels," this brings to mind David's instructions to Solomon on the temple equipment in 1 Chr 28:11–18 and the listing of the temple vessels in Ezra 1:7–10. When Simon is praised for "crushing the kings in those days," this could echo Ps 110:5–6: "He [God] will shatter kings on the day of his wrath . . . he will strike leaders throughout the land."

4QApocryphal Psalm and Prayer

pp. 112–15.

Only the beginning of this scroll, three columns, was preserved, with the thong used for binding the scroll. On the upper half of the scroll the beginning of a hymn referring to Zion was inscribed (col. 1)—and King Jonathan (=Jannaeus) indeed ruled from Zion. The hymn trusts in God that he will rescue Jerusalem and his people from their enemies. On the lower part of the scroll, a second scribe had written the blessing of King Jonathan—the first column and the beginning of the second are preserved (cols. 2–3)—and we do not know how long this text originally was.

This blessing testifies to messianic connotations connected to the Hasmonean kingdom. The praise of God's kingdom in column 2 is echoed in the blessing on the Judean kingdom in column 3. The text sees Jannaeus's wars, territorial expansion, and ingathering of the exiles as fulfillment of biblical promises such as Ezek 34:12–13; Mic 5:4–6; Zech 2:10–14. The reference to the assembly of Israel spread with the four winds of heaven connects Jannaeus with the ingathering of the exiles—see e.g. Zech 2:10: "Up, up! Flee from the land of the north, says the Lord, for I have scattered you to the four winds of heaven." Zech 2:10–12 refers to Zion, as does column 1 of 4Q448.

Jannaeus was the fourth of the great Maccabean rulers (Jonathan [160–142], Simon [142–134], John Hyrcanus [134–104], Alexander Jannaeus [104–76]). He was succeeded by his widow, the popular queen Salome Alexandra. Jannaeus ruled his nation with a mighty hand. In 88 BCE he made war on the Pharisees who had supported a coup trying to bring down his rule and crucified eight hundred Pharisees around Jerusalem while feasting with his concubines (Josephus, *Antiquities* 13:380).

For Further Reading

Eshel, Hanan. *Dead Sea Scrolls and the Hasmonean State*, 101–15.

Psalms of Solomon 17

pp. 116–19.

The hymn abounds with echoes of Davidic texts (Pss 2; 72; 110; 2 Sam 5:2; Jer 23:5–6; Isa 9:6; 11:1–5; Zech 9:9–10) and oracles of the future of Zion (Isa 2:1–5; 60:3–6). The messiah is a central actor in God's redemption of Zion. He appears as a mediator of God's presence and blessings, as the king is portrayed in Ps 72. The psalm recasts the role of the Davidic king as described in Ps 72:1–14, and the messiah's powerful role vis-à-vis other nations, as in Ps 2:8–12 and Ps 110.

The king is declared to be "free from sin" (seventh stanza), which does not mean that he is created different from other human beings—with the anthropology reflected in the Psalms of Solomon he belongs to those Israelites who are righteous and confide in their God.

For Further Reading

Elgvin, Torleif. *Warrior, King, Servant, Savior*, 258–62.

4QMessianic Apocalypse

pp. 120–22.

This scroll was copied around 100 BCE. The text was likely authored sometime during the second half of the second century. The text does not bear features characteristic of the Union and is heavily dependent on biblical passages. The text quoted here is not the beginning of the scroll, at least one column of text preceded it.

The passage should be read as a midrash on Dan 7, Ps 146, and 1 Sam 2. Line 1 makes the text a clear sequel to Dan 7:13–14, as it attributes universal lordship to "his anointed one," the princely messiah. Whatever the original meaning of "son of humankind" in Dan 7, here this figure is read as the end-time messiah. Daniel 7:13–14 is read as a heavenly inauguration of Israel's Davidic messiah.

The term "rules of the holy angels" (literally: "rules of the holy ones," line 2) indicates that the angels are mediators of the commandments that have their source in God and/or the messiah. While the messiah is the central figure in lines 1–3, God himself is the acting subject in lines 4–14, which closely follow Ps 146:7–10, read as a prophecy of the messianic age. However, the mighty deeds that God will do on earth belong to the days of the messiah. The object of the sentence "when you serve him" in line 3 is more likely the messiah than God; compare "obey his anointed" (line 1) and all nations serving the Son of Man in Dan 7:14.

In Dan 7:9–14, the focus is the reign given to the Son of Man, while in 7:15–27, it is the restoration of the people of God and the reign given to it by divine intervention. This twofold structure recurs in 4Q521, where lines 1–3 have the messiah in focus, while lines 4–14 describe how God will restore and redeem the elect community. The Son of Man/son of humankind is not mentioned in Dan 7:15–27, neither is the messiah in 4Q521, lines 4–14. In 4Q521, the enthronement of a messiah in heaven will lead to a renewal of God's people on earth.

For Further Reading

Elgvin, Torleif. *Warrior, King, Servant, Savior*, 200–202.

Justnes, Årstein. *The Time of Salvation: An Analysis of 4QApocryphon of Daniel ar (4Q246), 4QMessianic Apocalypse (4Q521 2), and 4QTime of Righteousness (4Q215a)*, 179–280. Frankfurt: Lang, 2009.

The Messianic Rule, 1QSa

pp. 123–24.

To the "library copy" of the Community Rule were added two appendices written by the same scribe as the larger text, the first usually called the Rule of the Congregation. Geza Vermes's suggested designation, the Messianic Rule, is more fitting. 1QSa was almost completely preserved on two columns, while the five columns of the last appendix, the Rule of Benedictions (pp. 125–29) had fared badly. 1QSa was also found in a fragmentary copy in Cave 4, written in cryptic script.

Zech 4 envisions two anointed ones standing before the heavenly Lord, a priestly and a royal leader. This text became formative for the hope of a priestly messiah or the idea of two messiahs alongside each other in the end-time.

The Messianic Rule is an early text, perhaps authored around the mid-second century. In the copies of the Community Rule we encounter the Community as God's chosen actor on earth = a collective messianism. When the library copy 1QS was edited around 100 BCE and the scribe was asked to include both a long psalmic text and the two appendices, one chose to add a reference to two messiahs also in the Community Rule immediately after a declaration of the Union as the spiritual temple and God's sanctified men, those who would prepare the way for the messianic times. The Cave 4 copy of this passage lacks this clause about two messiahs.

> At that time, the men of the Union shall set apart a holy house for Aaron, to form a most holy community and a house of communion for Israel . . . the men of holiness . . . shall be ruled by the original precepts by which the men of the Union were first instructed, until there shall come the prophet and the anointed ones of Aaron and Israel. (1QS 9:5–6, 8–11)

In accordance with the end-time hope of the Messianic Rule (1QSa), the clause added to the instructions of 1QS 9 specifies that there will be a priestly messiah and a royal messiah, the anointed of Aaron in pair with the anointed of Israel, and they will be announced by the end-time prophet. In a similar vein, the exegetical text 4QTestimonia (4Q174) expects three end-time figures, prophet, priest, and ruler.

4QApocryphon of Levi

pp. 130–31.

Written in Aramaic, scholars usually classify 4Q541 as a "pre-Qumranic" writing. The full text may have been formed as a "Levi testament." In this literary genre we are set at the deathbed of a biblical patriarch, who gives admonitions to his sons and their descendants and "prophecies" about the end-time.

This text brings us close to priestly hopes around Maccabean times. A hope that includes all mankind, not only the people of Israel. The Levitical priest of the end-time will teach powerfully, "his words are like the words of heaven, his teaching like the will of God."

When the priest makes atonement for all his generation, the setting may be the eschatological day of atonement in the Jerusalem temple. Heaven and earth meet in the temple, and Israel's high priest has an essential role in the renewal of the world. "Make atonement" means carrying a sacrificial animal into God's presence. Different from Isa 53, the text does not signal the sacrifice of the life of the priest. His ministry will have cosmic consequences, the godlike teaching and sacrificial ministry of the priest will open for a cosmic renewal.

The second paragraph of this visionary text must refer to a period before the breakthrough of universal renewal. There is internal strife in the people, the priest is controversial and a victim of slandering and probably persecution. Are the 170s seen as a blueprint for the end times? Could the high priest Onias III, who was killed by his enemies in 175 BCE, be some kind of type for this figure, or perhaps his son Onias IV, who found refuge in Egypt and built a new temple for the Lord in Heliopolis?

Isa 53 plays in the background. "Be sent to all the children of his people" recalls the "we-group" of Isa 53. "In his days the people will go astray" echoes "all we like sheep have gone astray" (53:6). "They will speak against him many words and many [lie] s, invent fables about him, and speak all kinds of shameful things about him" recalls "he was despised and rejected by men . . . he was despised, and we did not recognize him" (53:3). In another fragment of 4Q541 the text runs, "you will grow and see and rejoice in eternal light"—an echo of "through his soul's anguish he shall see light" (Isa 53:11, reading "light" with 1QIsa^{a,b}, 4QIsa^{d}, and the Greek text).

There is no son of David in the eschatological hope of 4Q541. The priest is God's only agent, as may be expected in a patriarchal testament coming out of priestly circles, four hundred years after the collapse of the House of David. The author may have found the motive of opposition, trials, suffering, and atonement in Isa 50 and 53, the central role of the priestly leader in Ezek 40–48, and his role in redemption in Jer 30:18–24 and Zech 13:7–9.

Elgvin, Torleif. "Trials and Universal Renewal—the Priestly Figure of the Levi Testament 4Q541." In *Vision, Narrative, and Wisdom in the Aramaic Texts from Qumran: Essays from the Copenhagen Symposium 14–15 August, 2017*, edited by Mette Bundvad and Kasper Siegismund, 78–100. Studies on the Texts of the Desert of Judah 131. Leiden: Brill, 2019.

———. *Warrior, King, Servant, Savior*, 241–44.

Self-Glorification Hymn

pp. 132–33.

This text is preserved in two recensions in four manuscripts: two copies of the Thanksgiving Hymns and two texts from the War Scroll tradition (1QH[a] 25–26; 4QH[a] [4Q427] 7 col. 1; 4Q491 11; 4Q471b). The text rendered here is from 4Q491, which has its own recension.

The singer knows he is elevated to the heavens and standing with the angels, "the sons of the king," before God's heavenly throne. The first editor of the text suggested that the imagined speaker was the archangel Michael.

However, the singer has teaching on earth included in his job description and has gone through trials and suffering. This would not fit the tasks of an angel—a priestly singer is a better solution. The imagined singer could be the Qumranites' founding father, the priest called the Teacher of Righteousness. Or, it could be the end-time messianic high priest, described in terms that at the same time would fit the Teacher. An officiating priest could be conceived as being spiritually connected with the heavenly sanctuary, see the text on pp. 127–28.

When the Qumran community was reciting this song in their liturgy, the members would imagine a similar union with the heavenly realms, including a hope of an ultimate partaking in the angelic song in the afterlife.

The songs of the Suffering Servant in Isa 50 and 53 have colored the stanzas that describe suffering and trials. One may draw lines from this text to New Testament application of the Servant Songs to Jesus as well as texts about Jesus' elevation to God's right hand.

For Further Reading

Elgvin, Torleif. *Warrior, King, Servant, Savior*, 244–49.

Testament of Levi

pp. 134–36.

Since a renowned article by Jacob Jervell ("Ein Interpolator interpretiert," 1969), many scholars recognize a Jewish-Christian editorial hand in the Testaments of the Twelve Patriarchs around the mid-second century, extending an earlier Jewish collection of patriarchal testaments. The designation "saints" for the believers is indebted to New Testament letters. The assertion that "the priesthood will come to an end" reflects a time after the fall of the temple. Similarly, "heaven will be opened, from the glorious temple above he will be sanctified by a fatherly voice, and the glory of the Most High will be poured upon him" would point to the gospels' depiction of the baptism of Jesus. The Matthean phrase, "this is my son, my beloved" is indeed quoting God's words to Abraham about Isaac (Gen 22:2), as it is expressed in the third stanza.

The Testament of Levi has the longest pre-history within the Testaments of the Twelve Patriarchs. It has many parallels with the Qumran text Aramaic Levi, preserved in two fragmentary manuscripts. The core of Aramaic Levi goes back to pre-Maccabean times, perhaps as early as the third century.

Aramaic Levi stresses the purity of the priest and attaches the roles of sage and scribe to the priesthood. The author was engaged in polemic against some form of the priesthood and in promotion of his own notion of the office's proper character. This elevation of Levi and the priesthood would hardly allow for a dual leadership with priest and son of David alongside each other, as in Zech 4 and early Qumran messianism (see pp. 101, 123–24, 208–9). The Qumranite Union nevertheless preserved Aramaic Levi as an expression of their self-definition and negative assessment of the Hasmonean high priesthood.

Different from Aramaic Levi, in the later Testament of Levi the patriarch is commissioned as priest and warrior. This tendenz suggests that, with Aramaic Levi as a main source, another recension was composed as an apology for the dual offices of Hasmonean rulers, perhaps in the time of John Hyrcanus (134–35).

For further reading

Kugler, Robert A. *From Patriarch to Priest: The Levi-Priestly Tradition from Aramaic Levi to Testament of Levi.* Atlanta: Scholars, 1996.

11QMelchizedek and Hebrews

pp. 137–38.

Three priestly writings from Qumran, from the second and first centuries BCE, describe Melchizedek as a main actor in the end-time drama (Visions of Amram, Songs of the Sabbath Sacrifice, 11QMelchizedek). Melchizedek is the leader of God's heavenly armies against the forces of Belial. He is the acting redeemer, while the elect community on earth appears as a more passive recipient of salvation. An analogous picture of Melchizedek emerges in 2 Enoch, a Jewish apocalypse from the late first century CE (2 Enoch 23).

11QMelchizedek was copied around 75–50 BCE. A priestly scribe lays out his expectation of the last days through a commentary on select biblical passages, first of the year of Jubilee (Lev 25:13), paired with Deut 15:2 on "a remission of God."

Following biblical texts (e.g., Ps 8:6) that use *'elohim* for angelic beings, the commentary interprets *'elohim* of Ps 82:1 and *El*, the divine judge of Ps 7:8, as God's second-in-command, Melchizedek. The proclamation "your *'elohim* has been made king" (Isa 52:7) is read about Melchizedek, not the Lord, and "the year of *'elohim's* favor" (Isa 61:2) is rendered as "the year of favor of Melchizedek." Melchizedek appears as the semidivine redeemer, chief of the heavenly armies, who leads the battle against the evil powers.

Melchizedek is instrumental when, during the end-time Day of Atonement, "atonement will be made for all the sons of [light]"—a climax of his performing bloodless Yom Kippur sacrifices above, accompanying the earthly sacrifices in the temple below. Melchizedek executes the end-time judgment on the evil forces and redeems the elect "sons of light," those who are of the "lot of Melchizedek."

11QMelchizedek likely quoted from Gen 14 and Ps 110, although such references are not preserved. Ps 110:1–4 was probably read as an address by God to Melchizedek, closing with "on my decree you are priest forever, Melchizedek."

The idea of a heavenly Melchizedek probably crystallized in priestly exegesis of Gen 14:18–20 and Ps 110:4 before the formation of the Qumranite Union. The names of Abraham's antagonists were read symbolically: the king of Gomorra, Birsha', was read as "son of wickedness," while the king of Sodom, Bera' was read as "son of evil" (Gen 14:2). Such a reading facilitated the understanding of Melchizedek as heavenly warrior fighting against evil powers. Gen 14 was then read as an earthly visit by the priestly angel Melchizedek, who helped Abraham in his fight against the evil powers, an interpretation probably shared by the letter to the Hebrews.

As I read the texts, Hebrews—itself a priestly/Levitical treatise—should be read in line with the tradition of these priestly texts. Hebrews 5:6, 10; 6:20 introduce Melchizedek as antetype of Jesus as end-time high priest, before the theme is unfolded in Heb 7: Melchizedek is "without father or mother . . . without beginning of days and end of life, like the Son of God he remains priest forever"; in contrast to earthly priests who are mortal, he is "declared to be living" (7:3, 8)—features that prefigure Jesus. Jesus appears as a priest like Melchizedek, not because of his ancestry (he was not of the tribe of Levi), but "on the power of an indestructible life" (7:15–16). And Jesus is proclaimed "priest forever, according to the order of Melchizedek" (5:10; 6:20).

Hebrews 2:10–18 portrays Jesus in conflict with the devil and sent to redeem the enslaved. The author likely draws on the tradition of Melchizedek as heavenly warrior and redeemer of the elect. As is the case in 11QMelchizedek, Hebrews reinterprets the atoning rituals of Yom Kippur in terms of eschatological redemption, making the temple rituals disposable. Thus, the author of Hebrews connected the Melchizedek tradition and the Jesus event: the angelic Melchizedek prefigures the priestly ministry of Jesus who brought himself forth as a sacrifice, concurrently on earth and in the heavenly sanctuary (9:24). As the heavenly Melchizedek once had a short sojourn on earth, so Christ descended from above so that he for a short time was positioned lower than the angels (2:6–9).

For Further Reading

Elgvin, Torleif. "Melchizedek." In *The Dead Sea Scrolls*, edited by Craig A. Evans and Cecilia Wassén. Ancient Literature for New Testament Studies. Vol. 3. Grand Rapids: Zondervan Academic, 2024 (forthcoming).

———. *Warrior, King, Servant, Savior*, 252–55.

Book of Giants

pp. 147–48.

The Enochic Book of Giants has been known from Manichean writings found in the Far East. In recent times, seven fragmentary copies of the Aramaic original were found in Qumran. It is a retelling of the Book of Watchers (1 Enoch 1–36), which wants to give a clearer answer to the question why evil exists in the world and among men: it was the fallen angels who brought evil upon the earth (Gen 6:1–4). When God sent the flood, he destroyed the rebellious angels and their offspring, the giants. However, the giants survived as evil spirits who inspire men to evil deeds. God has in principle defeated these spiritual forces, and he will soon appear as triumphant over them.

Some scholars have argued that in Qumran, the Book of Giants was included in an Enochic pentateuch (five books together). However, as retelling of the central core of 1 Enoch, the Book of Watchers, it would give more meaning if it was seen as a separate book that told another part of the career of Enoch the heavenly sage. Therefore, it was not included in the later translations of 1 Enoch to Greek and Ethiopic, and from the second or third century it was cherished by the Manicheans.

Sirach 35

pp. 149–50.

The Hebrew text of Sir 35:22–23 is more dualistic than Ben Sira's theology as we encounter it elsewhere in his book. He was an early Judean teacher who gives catechetic advice for this life. End-time scenarios and spiritual warfare were hardly part of his world view.

The verses speak about "the scepter of the scoffer" and "the staff of evil." This stanza may have been polished and updated in circles with a more apocalyptic view of the forces of evil and demonic powers, who saw such forces coming to the fore through the Syrian king Antiochus Epiphanes or his successors, the Roman empire that conquered the land and twice crushed the people of Judea in their revolts. The Qumran community is one of the candidates for this recension of Sirach 35.

The Qumran movement were not the only Judeans who asked God to break the staff of evil. When the daily liturgy for the High Holy Days was formulated sometime after the fall of the temple, one included a similar prayer that petitioned God to "remove the kingdom of evil from the earth." The Jerusalem scholar David Flusser argued that the rabbis here found an earlier prayer against the spiritual evil forces and gave it an edge toward the blasphemous Roman empire that had destroyed the temple of the Lord, at the same time keeping the cosmic-eschatological meaning of this prayer. In parallel, the daily prayer of Eighteen benedictions (the Amidah) was formulated in the first generations after the fall of the temple. By the mid-second century, Judean rabbis added a nineteenth prayer (more a curse than a benediction of praise), petitioning God to let the heretics perish and "uproot the kingdom of evil in our days"—with the "kingdom of evil" they clearly had the Roman empire in mind.

Jesus as well taught his disciples to pray to be delivered from evil, and for the kingdom of God soon to appear in full measure.

For Further Reading

Flusser, David. "'The Book of the Mysteries' and the High Holy Days Liturgy." In *Judaism of the Second Temple Period*. Vol. 1. *Qumran and Apocalypticism*. Translated by Azzan Yadin, 119–39. Grand Rapids: Eerdmans, 2007.

The "Son of God" text, 4QApocryphon of Daniel, 4Q246

pp. 151–53.

This scroll was penned two-three decades before the turn of the era, the text was likely composed in Aramaic in the early Maccabean period. Few Qumran texts have been so intensively discussed as this one. Is "the son of God" a messianic figure or a boasting blasphemous king (1:7—2:1)? Is the victorious subject in the last paragraph a royal messiah or the people of God (2:4–9)?

In my view, the parallels with Dan 7:7–8, 15–27 indicate that the main figure in 1:5—2:1 is neither a messiah nor a heavenly being (both options had their advocates among the scholars), but rather an ungodly king. The boasting king is modeled on Antiochus Epiphanes, but also has features of an "antichrist." In second- and early first-century texts (the Greek translation of Isaiah and Qumran biblical commentaries), the Isaianic term "king of Assyria" is reinterpreted as the Seleucid kings ruling from Syria and concretely as Antiochus Epiphanes.

4Q246 2:1–3 refers to the political struggles among the Seleucids and between the Seleucids and Ptolemies in the third and early second century. The rise and fall of these earthly kingdoms are likened with meteors that appeared in the king's vision: the "career" of a meteor rapidly changes, it shines brightly on the heavens but will soon collapse. At the end of 2:2 I restore (with Justnes 2009, 129–31) the Aramaic phrase *shany['a]*, "changing," not *shani[n]*, "years."

4Q246 is often called "The Son of God text." The parallels with the words of annunciation in Luke 1:32–35 do not make the ruler of 4Q246 1:4—2:1 a messiah (here I disagree with scholars such as John J. Collins and Richard Bauckham). They rather demonstrate the closeness of Luke's messianic terminology to royal ideology in the ancient Near East. The gospels were written at a time when the imperial cult was intensified, not the least in the eastern parts of the Roman Empire. Luke's words of annunciation relate to Davidic texts in the Bible. But this text, as many others in the gospels, vibrates with tension vis-à-vis Roman imperial ideology. Thus, 4Q246 remains important for the interpretation of Luke 1:32–35 and New Testament proclamation of Jesus as messiah.

4Q246 2:4–9 presents an interpretative crux. The earthly actor who has God as his strength is consistently referred to with a singular suffix—its/his, which can be read either as a divinely blessed king or the end-time people of God. My translation follows the latter option. Line 4 opens with a section marker (an empty space), which indicates the new era, the restoration of the people of God. The text of col. 2 is complete, no king or messiah is introduced before lines 4–9 elaborate on the end-time kingdom given to God's people. As in Dan 7:15–27, the people of God, which has been through turmoil and suffering, emerges as the victor of the end time. In this text, the restored people of the end-time is portrayed as the "messianic" community on earth, reflecting a collective messianism.

For Further Reading

Elgvin, Torleif. *Warrior, King, Servant, Savior*, 207–10.

Justnes, Årstein. *Time of Salvation*, 29–178.

War Scroll

pp. 156–58.

The War Scroll was found almost completely preserved in Qumran Cave 1 in 1947 (whether the other large "Cave 1 scrolls" indeed were found in the same Cave 1, later identified by the archaeologists, remains an open question). Later, six copies of the War Scroll (or its cousins) were found in Cave 4. The War Scroll seems to have gone through a long process of literary growth, from the second century to around the turn of the era.

The book deals with the end-time war between the sons of light and the sons of darkness—both within the people of Israel and among the gentiles. It deals particularly with the war against the enemy nation that has oppressed Israel. Early on, it was the Syrians with Antiochus Epiphanes who appeared in the role of the enemy. In the later version, the one preserved to us, the enemy troops carry Roman insignia and banners of war.

There are different literary genres within the book: formation of troops, depictions of the forces, blessings by the field chaplains, praises to God who will give his people victory. The field chaplain has a central role, while the book only in passing mentions the messianic leader of the troops, "the prince of all the congregation" (5:1). Thus, the book reflects a collective messianism, the elect community on earth is God's tool during the birth pangs of the end-time.

The dualistic and aggressive ideas we encounter in the War Scroll may explain why Essenes joined the great revolt against the Romans—Josephus refers to a rebel commander called John the Essene. Essenes joined forces with Judeans they earlier had detested, to drive the blasphemous enemy out of God's chosen land. Even to Masada, the last outpost of the revolt, did Essenes find their way.

It is commonly held that the New Testament message is different and peaceful. However, in Rev 8–18 there are texts on the end-time reminiscent of passages in the War Scroll. John of Patmos had possibly personally seen how the Roman armies slaughtered Judeans when they invaded Judea, he knew how the emperor Nero had persecuted Christians, and how Christians who refused to worship emperor Domitian as divine could risk being executed in Asia Minor in the 90s. For John, the Roman empire was demonic in character. This prophetic-exegetical book with its strong apocalyptic color reflects a dualistic world view analogous to that of the War Scroll, with the angels in heaven partaking in the cosmic battle against demonic forces, and the angels being allied with God's community on earth. The designation "sons of light"—the self-designation of the Qumranite Union, would soon be "occupied" by New Testament authors (John 12:36; Eph 5:8).

For Further Reading

Brent Nongbri. "How the 'Jerusalem Scrolls' Became the Dead Sea Scrolls from Qumran Cave 1: Archaeology, the Antiquities Market, and the Spaces in Between." *Harvard Theological Review* 115 (2022) 1–22.

Schultz, Brian. "Milhamah (M)." In *T&T Clark Companion to the Dead Sea Scrolls*, 322–24.

Yadin, Yigael. *The Scroll of the War of the Sons of Light Against the Sons of Darkness: Edited with Commentary and Introduction by Yigael Yadin.* London: Oxford University Press, 1962.

4QTime of Righteousness

pp. 159–60

Themes from this text recur in the New Testament: God's kingdom is close at hand (Mark 1:15). His plan of salvation was decided eternally (Eph 1:3–14; 3:9). God elects a community in the last days and tests his chosen ones (1 Pet 1:6–7). All nations shall bow down before God's throne (Isa 45:23; Phil 2:9–11). Another small fragment of the scroll gives God's holy spirit a central role in creation. This text represents a *collective* messianism, the elect community becomes a tool for the renewal of all mankind.

According to the universal hope of 4Q215a, all mankind "will be] of on[e hea]rt." This line echoes Ezek 11:19, which tells that God will renew his people and give them "one heart and a new spirit." The Qumran text extends this to a promise for all mankind. Also the early Jesus movement professed they were all "of one heart" (Acts 4:32), as a fulfilment of Ezekiel's prophecy. (While the Syriac and some Hebrew manuscripts read "a new heart and a new spirit"—my preferred reading of the Hebrew text of Ezekiel.)

For Further Reading

Elgvin, Torleif. "The Eschatological Hope of 4QTime of Righteousness." In *Wisdom and Apocalypticism in the Dead Sea Scrolls and in the Biblical Tradition,* edited by Florentino García Martínez, 89–102. Bibliotheca Ephemeridum theologicarum Lovaniensium *168*. Leuven: Peeters, 2003.

Bibliography

Translations and Editions Consulted

Bauckham, Richard, et al., eds. *Old Testament Pseudepigrapha: More Noncanonical Scriptures.* vol. 1. Grand Rapids: Eerdmans, 2013. [vol. 2, 2025.]

Charlesworth, James H., ed. *The Old Testament Pseudepigrapha.* 2 vols. New York: Doubleday, 1983, 1985.

Fink, Uta Barbara. *Joseph und Aseneth. Revision des griechischen Textes und Edition der zweiten lateinischen Übersetzung.* Fontes et subsidia ad Bibliam Pertinentes 5. Berlin: de Gruyter, 2008.

García Martínez, Florentino, and Eibert J. C. Tigchelaar, eds. *The Dead Sea Scrolls Study Edition.* 2 vols. Leiden: Brill, 1997, 1998.

The Jerusalem Bible. London: Darton, Longman & Todd, 1966.

Nickelsburg, George W. E. *1 Enoch 1. A Commentary on the Book of 1 Enoch, Chapters 1–36; 81–108.* Hermeneia. Minneapolis: Fortress, 2001.

Pietersma, Albert, and Benjamin G. Wright, eds and trans. *A New English Translation of the Septuagint.* Oxford: Oxford University Press, 2007.

Schuller, Eileen M., and Carol A. Newsom. *The Hodayot (Thanksgiving Psalms): A Study Edition of 1QH^{a}*. Early Judaism and Its Literature 36. Atlanta: SBL, 2012.

VanderKam, James C., trans. *Jubilees: The Hermeneia Translation.* Hermeneia. Minneapolis: Fortress, 2020.

Vermes, Geza, ed. and trans. *The Complete Dead Sea Scrolls in English.* London: Lane/Penguin, 1997.

Wise, Michael O., et al., trans. *The Dead Sea Scrolls: A New Translation.* San Francisco: HarperSanFrancisco, 1996.

Wright, Robert B., ed. *The Psalms of Solomon: A Critical Edition of the Greek Text.* Jewish and Christian Texts in Contexts and Related Studies 1. New York: T. & T. Clark, 2007.

General Introductions

Bauckham, Richard, and James R. Davila. "Introduction." In *Old Testament Pseudepigrapha: More Noncanonical Scriptures*, vol. 1:xvii–xxviii. Grand Rapids: Eerdmans, 2013.

Crawford, Sidnie White. *Scribes and Scrolls at Qumran*. Grand Rapids: Eerdmans, 2019.

DeSilva, David A. *Introducing the Apocrypha: Message, Context, and Significance*. 2nd ed. Grand Rapids: Baker Academic, 2018.

Elgvin, Torleif. *Warrior, King, Servant, Savior: Messianism in the Hebrew Bible and Early Jewish Texts*. Grand Rapids: Eerdmans, 2022.

Lim, Timothy H. *The Dead Sea Scrolls. A Very Short Introduction*. Very Short Introductions. Oxford: Oxford University Press, 2017.

Metzger, Bruce M. *An Introduction to the Apocrypha*. New York: Oxford University Press, 1957. Reprint, 1963.

Perrin, Andrew B. *Lost Words and Forgotten Worlds of the Dead Sea Scrolls*. Lexham, UK: Lexham, forthcoming.

Society of Biblical Literature, ed. *The SBL Study Bible. New Revised Standard Version. Updated Edition, with the Apocryphal/Deuterocanonical Books*. New York: HarperOne, 2023.

Wills, Lawrence M. *Introduction to the Apocrypha: Jewish Books in Christian Bibles*. New Haven: Yale University Press, 2021.

Studies Relating to Specific Texts

Adams, Samuel, et al., eds. *Sirach and Its Contexts*. Journal for the Study of Judaism Supplements 196. Leiden: Brill, 2021.

Askin, Lindsey A. *Scribal Culture in Ben Sira*. Supplements to the Journal for the Study of Judaism 184. Leiden: Brill, 2018.

Atkinson, Kenneth. *A History of the Hasmonean State: Josephus and Beyond*. Jewish and Christian Texts in Contexts and Related Studies 23. London: Bloomsbury T. & T. Clark, 2016.

Berlin, Andrea M., and Paul J. Kosmin, eds. *The Middle Maccabees: Archaeology, History, and the Rise of the Hasmonean Kingdom*. Archaeology and Biblical Studies 28. Atlanta: SBL Press, 2021.

Bohak, Gideon. *Joseph and Aseneth and the Jewish Temple in Heliopolis*. Early Judaism and Its Literature 10. Atlanta: Scholars, 1996.

Brooke, George J., and Charlotte Hempel, eds. *T. & T. Clark Companion to the Dead Sea Scrolls*. T. & T. Clark Companions. London: T. & T. Clark, 2019.

Doran, Robert. *2 Maccabees: A Critical Commentary*. Hermeneia. Minneapolis: Fortress, 2012.

Elgvin, Torleif. "The Eschatological Hope of 4QTime of Righteousness." In *Wisdom and Apocalypticism in the Dead Sea Scrolls and in the Biblical Tradition*, edited by Florentino García Martínez, 89–102. Bibliotheca Ephemeridum theologicarum Lovaniensium 168. Leuven: Peeters, 2003.

———. "From the Earthly to the Heavenly Temple: Lines from the Bible and Qumran to Hebrews and Revelation." In *The World of Jesus and the Early Church: Identity and Interpretation in Early Communities of Faith*, edited by Craig A. Evans, 23–36. Peabody, MA: Hendrickson, 2011.

———. *The Literary Growth of the Song of Songs during the Hasmonean and Early-Herodian Periods*. Contributions to Biblical Exegesis and Theology 28. Leuven: Peeters, 2018.

———. "Melchizedek." In *The Dead Sea Scrolls*, edited by Craig A. Evans and Cecilia Wassén. Ancient Literature for New Testament Studies 3. Grand Rapids: Zondervan Academic, forthcoming.

———. "Priests on Earth as in Heaven: Jewish Light on the Book of Revelation." In *Echoes From the Caves: Qumran and the New Testament*, edited by Florentino García Martínez, 257–78. Studies on the Texts of the Desert of Judah 85. Leiden: Brill, 2009.

———. "The Song of Songs: Torah, Creation, Celebration, and Libertinism." In *Between Wisdom and Torah: Discourses on Wisdom and Law in Second Temple Judaism*, edited by Jiseong J. Kwon and Seth A. Bledsoe, 243–74. Deuterocanonical and Cognate Literature Studies 51. Berlin: de Gruyter, 2023.

———. "Trials and Universal Renewal—the Priestly Figure of the Levi Testament 4Q541." In *Vision, Narrative, and Wisdom in the Aramaic Texts from Qumran*, edited by Mette Bundvad and Kasper Siegismund, 78–100. Studies on the Texts of the Desert of Judah 131. Leiden: Brill, 2019.

Eshel, Hanan. *The Dead Sea Scrolls and the Hasmonean State*. Studies in the Dead Sea Scrolls and Related Literature. Grand Rapids: Eerdmans, 2008.

Falk, Daniel K. "Barkhi Nafshi." In *T. & T. Clark Companion to the Dead Sea Scrolls*, edited by George J. Brooke and Charlotte Hempel, 286–88. T. & T. Clark Companions. London: T. & T. Clark, 2019.

———. "Daily Prayers." In *Outside the Bible: Ancient Jewish Writings Related to Scripture*, edited by Louis H. Feldman et al., 1927–38. 3 vols. Philadelphia: Jewish Publication Society, 2013.

———. "Festival Prayers." In *Outside the Bible: Ancient Jewish Writings Related to Scripture*, edited by Louis H. Feldman et al., 1939–59. 3 vols. Philadelphia: Jewish Publication Society, 2013.

———. "Words of the Luminaries." In *Outside the Bible: Ancient Jewish Writings Related to Scripture*, edited by Louis H. Feldman et al., 1960–84. 3 vols. Philadelphia: Jewish Publication Society, 2013.

Fitzmyer, Joseph A. *Tobit*. Commentaries on Early Jewish Literature. Berlin: de Gruyter, 2003.

Flusser, David. "'The Book of the Mysteries' and the High Holy Days Liturgy." In *Judaism of the Second Temple Period*. Vol. 1, *Qumran and Apocalypticism*, 119–39. Translated by Azzan Yadin. Grand Rapids: Eerdmans, 2007.

Gera, Deborah Levine. *Judith*. Commentaries on Early Jewish Literature. Berlin: de Gruyter, 2014.

Harkins , Angela Kim. "Hodayot (H)." In *T. & T. Clark Companion to the Dead Sea Scrolls*, edited by George J. Brooke and Charlotte Hempel, 314–18. T. & T. Clark Companions. London: T. & T. Clark, 2019.

Honigman, Sylvie. *Tales of High Priests and Taxes: The Books of the Maccabees and the Judean Rebellion against Antiochus IV*. Hellenistic Culture and Society 56. Berkeley: University of California Press, 2014.

Justnes, Årstein. *The Time of Salvation: An Analysis of 4QApocryphon of Daniel ar (4Q246), 4QMessianic Apocalypse (4Q521 2), and 4QTime of Righteousness (4Q215a)*. European University Studies. Series 23, Theology 893. Frankfurt: Peter Lang, 2009.

Kugler, Robert A. *From Patriarch to Priest: The Levi-Priestly Tradition from Aramaic Levi to Testament of Levi*. Early Judaism and Its Literature 9. Atlanta: Scholars, 1996.

Ma, John. "Re-Examining Hanukkah." *Marginalia Review of Books*, July 9, 2013. https://themarginaliareview.com/re-examining-hanukkah/.

Monger, Matthew. "The Many Forms of Jubilees. A Reassessment of the Manuscript Evidence from Qumran and the Lines of Transmission of the Parts and Whole of Jubilees," *Revue de Qumran* 30 (2018) 191–211.

———. "4Q216—A New Material Analysis," *Semitica* 60 (2018) 309–33.

Newman, Judith H. "Words of the Luminaries." In *T&T Clark Companion to the Dead Sea Scrolls*, edited by George J. Brooke and Charlotte Hempel, 365–66. T. & T. Clark Companions. London: T. & T. Clark, 2019.

Nongbri, Brent. "How the 'Jerusalem Scrolls' Became the Dead Sea Scrolls from Qumran Cave 1: Archaeology, the Antiquities Market, and the Spaces in Between." *Harvard Theological Review* 115 (2022) 1–22.

Rhyder, Julia. "Hellenizing Hanukkah: The Commemoration of Military Victory in the Books of the Maccabees." In: *Collective Violence and Memory in the Ancient Mediterranean*, edited by Sonja Ammann, Helge Bezold, Stephen Germany, and Julia Rhyder, 92–109. CHANE 135. Leiden: Brill, 2023.

Wills, Lawrence M. *Judith: A Commentary on the Book of Judith*. Hermeneia. Minneapolis: Fortress, 2019.

Yadin, Yigael. *The Scroll of the War of the Sons of Light against the Sons of Darkness*. Edited with Commentary and Introduction by Yigael Yadin. Translated from the Hebrew by Batya and Chaim Rabin. London: Oxford University Press, 1962.

www.ingramcontent.com/pod-product-compliance
Lightning Source LLC
Chambersburg PA
CBHW020406230426
43664CB00009B/1206
* 9 7 8 1 6 6 6 7 7 0 0 1 8 *